NIKOLAI GOGOL

Nikolai Gogol

BY VLADIMIR NABOKOV

A NEW DIRECTIONS PAPERBOOK

Library of Congress Catalog Card Number: 44–8135

ISBN: 978-0-8112-0120-9

MANUFACTURED IN THE UNITED STATES OF AMERICA

First published as ND Paperbook 78, 1959; corrected edition, 1961

New Directions Books are printed on acid-free paper.

Published in Canada by Penguin Books Canada Limited

NINETEENTH PRINTING

*New Directions Books are published
for James Laughlin
by New Directions Publishing Corporation,
80 Eighth Avenue, New York 10011.*

C O N T E N T S

NIKOLAI GOGOL

"No, I have not the strength to bear this any longer. God, the things they are doing to me! They pour cold water upon my head! They do not heed me, nor see me, nor listen to me. What have I done to them? Why do they torture me? What do they want of poor me? What can I give them? I have nothing. My strength is gone, I cannot endure all this torture. My head is aflame, and everything spins before my eyes. Save me, someone! Take me away. Give me three steeds, steeds as fast as the whirling wind! Seat yourself, driver, ring out, little harness bell, wing your way up, steeds, and rush me out of this world. On and on, so that nothing be seen of it, nothing. Yonder the sky wheels its clouds; a tiny star glitters afar; a forest sweeps by with its dark trees, and the moon comes in its wake; a silvergrey mist swims below; a musical string twangs in the mist; there is the sea on one hand, there is Italy on the other; and now Russian peasant huts can be discerned. Is that my home looming blue in the distance? Is that my mother sitting there at her window? Mother dear, save your poor son! Shed a tear upon his aching head. See, how they torture him. Press the poor orphan to your heart. There is no place for him in the whole wide world! He is a hunted creature. Mother dear, take pity on your sick little child. . . . And by the way, gentlemen, do you know that the Bey of Algiers has a round lump growing right under his nose?"

—Gogol; *Diary of a Madman*

1. HIS DEATH AND HIS YOUTH

1

NIKOLAI GOGOL, THE STRANGEST PROSE-POET RUSSIA EVER produced, died Thursday morning, a little before eight, on the fourth of March, eighteen fifty-two, in Moscow. He was almost forty-three years old—a reasonably ripe age for him, considering the ridiculously short span of life generally allotted to other great Russian writers of his miraculous generation. Absolute bodily exhaustion in result of a private hunger strike (by means of which his morbid melancholy had tried to counter the Devil) culminated in acute anemia of the brain (together, probably, with gastro-enteritis through inanition)—and the treatment he was subjected to, a vigorous purging and blood-letting, hastened the death of an organism already gravely impaired by the after effects of malaria and malnutrition. The couple of diabolically energetic physicians who insisted on treating him as if he were an average Bedlamite, much to the alarm of their more intelligent but less active colleagues, intended to break the back of their patient's insanity before attempting to patch up whatever bodily health he still had left. Some fifteen years before, Pushkin, with a bullet in his entrails, had been given medical assistance good for a constipated child. Second rate German and French general practitioners still dominated the scene, for the splendid school of great Russian physicians was yet in the making.

The learned doctors crowding around the Malade Imaginaire with their dog-Latin and gigantic belly-pumps cease to be funny when Molière suddenly coughs out his life-blood on the turbulent stage. It is horrible to read of the grotesquely rough handling that Gogol's poor limp body underwent when all he asked for was to be left in peace. With as fine a misjudgment of symptoms, as a clear anticipation of the methods of Charcot, Dr. Auvers (or Hovert) had his patient plunged into a warm bath where his head was soused with cold water after which he was put to bed with half-a-dozen plump leeches affixed to his nose. He had groaned and cried and weakly struggled while his wretched body (you could feel the spine through the stomach) was carried to the deep wooden bath; he shivered as he lay naked in bed and kept pleading to have the leeches removed: they were dangling from his nose and getting into his mouth (Lift them, keep them away, —he pleaded) and he tried to sweep them off so that his hands had to be held by stout Auvert's (or Hauvers's) hefty assistant.

Although the scene is unpleasant and has a human appeal which I deplore, it is necessary to dwell upon it a little longer in order to bring out the curiously physical side of Gogol's genius. The belly is the belle of his stories, the nose is their beau. His stomach had been his "noblest inner organ"—now it was practically gone and devils were dangling from his nostrils. In the months preceding his death he had starved himself so thoroughly that he had destroyed the prodigious capacity his stomach had once been blessed with; for none had sucked in such a number of macaroni or eaten so many cherry pies as this thin little man (one remembers the "plump little tummies" which he has given to his otherwise puny Dobchinsky and Bobchinsky in *The Government Inspector*). His big sharp nose was of such length and mobility that in the days of his youth he had been able (being something of an amateur contortionist), to bring its tip and his underlip in ghoulish contact; this nose was his keenest and most essential outer part. It was so sharp and long that it could "penetrate personally without the assistance of fingers into the smallest snuff-box, if of course a chiquenaude did not come to repel the intruder" (from one of Gogol's letters to a young lady—hence the archness). We shall meet the nasal leitmotiv throughout his imaginative work and it is hard to find any other author who has described with such gusto smells, sneezes and snores. This or that hero comes into the story trundling, as it were, his nose in a wheelbarrow—or drives in like the stranger in Slawkenburgius' tale in Sterne. There is an orgy of snufftaking. Chichikov, in *Dead Souls*, is introduced to the remarkable trumpet blast he emits when using his handkerchief. Noses drip, noses twitch, noses are lovingly or roughly handled; one drunkard attempts to *saw off* the nose of an-

3

other; the inhabitants of the moon (so a madman discovers) are Noses.

This nose-consciousness resulted at last in the writing of a story, *The Nose*, which is verily a hymn to that organ. A Freudian might suggest that in Gogol's topsy-turvy world human beings are turned upside down (in 1841 Gogol coolly declared that a council of doctors in Paris had found his stomach to be placed upside down) so that the part of the nose is played by some other organ and vice-versa. Whether the "fancy begat the nose or the nose begat the fancy" is inessential. I think it more reasonable to forget that Gogol's exaggerated concern with noses was based on the fact of his own being abnormally long and to treat Gogol's olfactivism—and even his own nose—as a literary trick allied to the broad humor of carnivals in general and to Russian nose-humor in particular. We are nose-gay and nose-sad. The display of nasal allusions in a famous scene of Rostand's *Cyrano de Bergerac* is nothing in comparison to the hundreds of Russian proverbs and sayings that revolve around the nose. We hang it in dejection, we lift it up in glory; slack memory is advised to make a notch in it and it is wiped for you by your victor. It is used as a measure of length when referring to some impending event of a more or less threatening nature. We speak of leading somebody by it or leaving somebody with it more than other nations do. The drowsy man "angles" with it instead of nodding. A big one is said to bridge the Volga or to have been growing for a century. A tingle inside it portends a piece of good news while a pimple on its tip means a coming carouse. Any writer alluding, say, to a fly settling on a man's nose used to earn in Russia thereby

4

the reputation of a humorist. In his juvenilia Gogol automatically followed this easy method but in his mature work he added to this the special touch of his queer genius. The point to be noted is that from the very start the nose *as such* was a funny thing to his mind (as to that of all Russians) something sticking out, something not quite belonging to its bearer, and at the same time (that much I may as well concede to the Freudians) something peculiarly and grotesquely masculine. It is almost painful the way Gogol has, when describing a pretty maiden, of dwelling upon the smooth egg-like quality of her face.

The fact remains that Gogol's long sensitive nose had discovered new smells in literature (which led to a new "frisson"). As a Russian saying goes "the man with the longest nose sees further"; and Gogol saw with his nostrils. The organ which in his juvenile work was but a carnival character borrowed from that cheap shop of ready-made clothes called "folklore," turned out to be at the climax of his genius his most important ally. When he destroyed his own genius by trying to become a preacher, he lost his nose just as Kovalyov lost his (in Gogol's *The Nose*).

This is why there is something dreadfully symbolic in the pathetic scene (which an eye-witness has recorded) of the futile attempts on the part of the dying man to get rid of the hideous black clusters of chaetopod worms sucking at his nostrils. We can imagine what he felt if we remember too that all his life he had been obsessed by a particular aversion to slimy, creeping, furtive things, and this aversion had a kind of religious basis. A scientific description of the geographic races of the Devil has not been attempted yet; the main characters of the Russian subspecies can be but briefly noted here. In its wriggly immature stage, which was the one in which Gogol mainly encountered him, the "Chort" is for good Russians a shrimpy foreigner, a shivering puny green-blooded imp with thin German, Polish, French legs, a sneaking little cad ("podlenky") with something inexpressibly repellent ("gadenky") about him. To squash him is a mixture of nausea and ecstasy; but so revolting is his squirming black essence that no force on earth could make one perform this business with the bare hand; and a shock of electric disgust darts up any instrument used, transforming the latter into a prolongation of one's very body. The arched back of a lean black cat or some harmless reptile with a throbbing throat, or again the slight limbs and slippery eyes of some petty rascal (who indeed was a rascal *because* he was scrawny) provoked Gogol in a special way owing to their "chort"-like features. That his devil was of the kind Russian drunkards see tends to minimize the worth of the religious experience which he enforced upon himself and upon others. There are many queer but harmless little gods that have scales, or claws, or even cloven hooves—but Gogol never realized this. As a child he strangled and buried a hungry and timorous cat not because he was naturally cruel, but because the slinking softness of the poor animal's body made his gorge rise. He told Pushkin one night that the funniest thing he had ever seen in his life was the sight of a tomcat progressing by fitful jumps along the redhot roof of a burning house— and indeed the sight of a devil dancing in anguish amid the very element where he was wont to torment human

6

souls must have seemed to hell-fearing Gogol an exquisitely comic paradox. A cold black caterpillar which chanced to touch the back of his hand as he was plucking some roses in Aksakov's garden sent him shrieking back to the house. In Switzerland, he had quite a field-day knocking the life out of the lizards all along the sunny mountain paths. The cane he used for this purpose may be seen in a daguerrotype of him taken in Rome in 1845. It is a very elegant affair.

2

He is shown in three quarters, holding that slim ivory-knobbed cane between the delicately shaped fingers of his writing hand (as if the cane were a pen). The long but well brushed hair is parted on the left side. A neat thin moustache surmounts the unpleasant lips. The nose is big and pointed, in keeping with the sharp features of the face. A dark shading remindful of that which used to surround the eyes of romantic characters in the old cinema pictures lends his gaze a sunken and slightly "haunted" expression. He wears a coat with ample lapels and a fancy waistcoat. And if the dim print of the past could burst into color we would see the bottle-green tint of that waistcoat

7

flecked with orange and amaranth, with the pleasing addition of minute dark-blue eyespots in between—on the whole resembling the skin of some exotic reptile.

3

His boyhood? Uninteresting. He passed through the usual illnesses: mumps, scarlet fever and *pueritus scribendi.* He was a weakling, a trembling mouse of a boy, with dirty hands and greasy locks, and pus trickling out of his ear. He gorged himself with sticky sweets. His schoolmates avoided touching the books he had been using. Upon completing his schooling at Nezhin in the Ukraine he left for St. Petersburg to look for some job. His arrival in the capital was marred by a bad cold which was all the more unpleasant through his not being able to feel his frost-bitten nose. Some three hundred and fifty roubles were immediately spent on new clothes—at least this is the sum he quotes in one of his dutiful letters to his mother. However, according to one of those legends that in after years Gogol was so good at weaving round his own past, the very first step he took straight upon his arrival was a visit to Pushkin whom he frantically admired without of course knowing the great poet personally. The great poet was still in bed and could not be seen. "Dear me," said Gogol with awe and sympathy, "he must have been working all night?" "Working indeed," snorted Pushkin's valet. "Playing cards, rather."

A rather desultory search for a job followed, vaguely punctuated with requests to his mother for money. He had brought to St. Petersburg a few poems, one of which was

8

a long and hazy affair called *Hanz* (sic!) *Kuechelgarten,* while another dealt with Italy.

> "Oh, Italy, luxuriant land,
>   For which my moaning spirit sighs,
>   All full of joy, all paradise,
>   Where Love, luxuriant Love vernates."

The verses are decidedly of a writer's vernating stage; still, a few striking lines do occur here and there, such as "A fiery traveler from an ice-bound land" or "Under the sun the wave tálks in her sleep."

The Kuechelgarten poem is about a mildly Byronic German student and contains such queer images, inspired from reading too many German moon-and-graveyard stories, as:

> "A white-shrouded dead man
>   Stretches himself out of his grave—
>   And solemnly wipes
>   The dust off his bones, atta boy!"

This jarring ejaculation is remarkable in the sense that one somehow feels young Gogol's Ukrainian spirits getting the better of German romanticism. There is not much else to be said about the poem which except for this delightful corpse is a complete and most dreadful failure. Written in 1827, it was published in 1829. Gogol, whom so many contemporaries have accused of being secretive and mysterious, may be excused this time for anxiously peering from behind a clumsy nom-de-plume (V. Alov)— to see what would happen next. What did happen was complete silence and then a short but devastating bit of criticism in the *Moscow Telegraph*. Gogol and his trusted servant rushed to the bookshops, bought up all the copies of *Hanz* and burned them. Thus Gogol's literary career began as it was to end some twenty years later with an auto da fé, and in both cases he was helped by an obedient though sorely puzzled serf.

What fascinated him in St. Petersburg? The numerous shop signs. What else? The fact that passers-by talked to themselves and "gesticulated in undertone" as they walked. Those that like following up this kind of thing may find it interesting to discover the shop-sign theme lavishly displayed in his later works and the mumbling pedestrians telescoped into Akaky Akakyevich of *The Overcoat*. These connections are a little too easy and thus probably false. Impressions do not make good writers; good writers make them up themselves in their youth and then use them as if they had been real originally. The shop signs in the St. Petersburg of the late twenties were painted and multiplied by Gogol himself in his letters in order to convey to his mother—and perhaps to his own imagination—the symbolic meaning of the "capital" as opposed to the "provincial towns" which she knew (where shop signs were of course just as fascinating—blue boots, criss-cross funnels of cloth, golden loaves of bread and other more sophisticated emblems which you will find in the beginning of *Dead Souls*). Symbolism with him took on a physiological aspect, in this case optical. The mutterings of passers-by were again symbolic, this time an auditory effect which was meant to render the hectic loneliness of a poor man in an opulent crowd. Gogol, and Gogol alone, spoke to himself as he walked, but the monologue was echoed and multiplied by the shadows of his mind. Passing as it were

10

through Gogol's temperament, St. Petersburg acquired a reputation of strangeness which it kept up for almost a century, losing it when it ceased to be the capital of an empire. The chief town in Russia had been built by a tyrant of genius upon a swamp, and upon the bones of slaves rotting in that swamp; this was the root of that strangeness—and the initial flaw. The Neva flooding the town had already been a kind of dim mythological vengeance (as Pushkin described it), the bog-gods trying to take back what belonged to them; and their tussle with the bronze Tsar was a vision which drove mad one of the first "petty officials" in Russian literature, the hero of Pushkin's *Bronze Horseman*. Pushkin had felt that something was wrong with St. Petersburg; had noticed the queer pale green tint of its skies and the mysterious energy of the bronze Tsar rearing his steed against a fluid background in a wilderness of wide streets and spacious squares. Its real strangeness, however, was probed and displayed when such a man as Gogol walked down Nevsky Avenue. The story bearing that title stressed the strangeness in such a vivid and unforgettable manner that Blok's poems and Bely's novel *Petersburg*—which belong to the dawn of this century—seem rather to develop Gogol's town than to create new images of its mystery. St. Petersburg was not quite real—but then Gogol, Gogol the ghoul, Gogol the ventriloquist, was not quite real either. As a schoolboy he would walk with perverse perseverance on the wrong side of the street, would wear the right shoe on the left foot, emit courtyard morning sounds in the middle of the night and distribute the furniture in his room according to a kind of Alice-in-the-Looking-Glass

11

logic. No wonder St. Petersburg revealed its oddity when the oddest Russian in Russia walked its streets. For St. Petersburg was just that: a reflection in a blurred mirror, an eerie medley of objects put to the wrong use, things going backwards the faster they moved forward, pale gray nights instead of ordinary black ones, and black days— the "black day" of a down-to-heel clerk. The door of a private house might open and a pig might come out—just like that. A man gets into a carriage, but he is not really a fat, sly, big-bottomed man—but your Nose—and this is the "transference of sense" so peculiar to dreams. A lighted window in a house turns out to be a hole in a crumbling wall. Your first and only love is a meretricious woman whose purity is a myth, and this myth is your life. "The sidewalk sped under him, the carriages with their swift horses seemed motionless, the bridge stretched out and broke in the middle of its arch, a house stood upside down, a sentry box toppled towards him, and the sentry's halberd, together with the golden letters of a shop sign and a pair of scissors painted thereon seemed to glitter on the very lash of his eye." There they are, the shop signs (*Nevsky Avenue*).

As an artist twenty years old Gogol was in exactly the right town for the development of his eccentric genius; as a jobless young man shivering in the mist of St. Petersburg, so dismally cold and gray in comparison with his Ukraine (a horn of plenty, bursting with fruit against a background of cloudless cobalt) he hardly could have felt happy. Still the sudden resolution which he took in the beginning of July 1829 has never been and never will be adequately explained by his biographers. Using some money which his mother had sent him for quite a different purpose he suddenly bolted abroad. All I can do is to note that after every shock he experienced during his literary career (and the flop of his sorry poem affected him as painfully as did a few years later the criticism directed against his immortal play) he would hurriedly leave whatever town he happened to be in. This feverish flight was only the first stage in the obscure persecution mania which scholars psychiatristically inclined decipher in his monstrous propensity for traveling. What actual data we have in respect of this first voyage show Gogol at his best, that is using his imagination for the purpose of complex and unnecessary deception. This is illustrated by letters to his mother telling her of his departure and journey.

4

At this point it behooves me to say a few words about that mother of his, although frankly speaking I am sick of reading biographies in which mothers are subtly deduced from the writing of their sons and then made to "influence" their remarkable sons in this or that way. It has been suggested that the fantastical, hysterical, superstitious and hypersuspicious, but still rather lovable Maria Gogol, had been responsible for inspiring Nikolai with that fear of hell which tormented him throughout his life; but probably we should be nearer the truth if we merely said that she and her son were temperamentally very much alike,— adding, perhaps, that this weird provincial lady who amazed or bored her friends by maintaining that railway engines, steamers and what not had been invented by her

Nikolai (and drove her son himself to the limits of irritation by coyly suggesting that he was the author of any
trashy novel that came her way) uncannily seems to the
reader of Gogol to be a child of Gogol's imagination. He
was so keenly aware of her deplorable literary tastes and
so averse to having her exaggerate his creative capacities
that after he became a writer he never alluded to his literary plans or labors in his letters to her although in the past
he had had her supply him with notes on Ukrainian customs and names. He saw little of her during the years in
which his genius grew. The cold contempt in which he
held her wits, her credulity, her inefficiency as a landowner is painfully apparent in his letters; but on the other
hand, owing to a smug semi-religious tradition, he never
failed to stress his filial devotion, his perfect obedience—
at least while he was still young—all this couched in a
highly sentimental and pompous style. Gogol's correspondence as a whole makes dreary reading, but the following letter to his mother is an exception.

(Having to give his mother an explanation of his sudden
departure he selected a reason that might appeal to her
romantic nature. In my translation I have tried to retain
something of the uncouth pomposity of this epistle.)

"Mother! I know not what will be your emotions when
you read my letter; all that I am aware of is that it will not
bring you peace. . . . To tell the truth, I think I have
never given you any joy that was wholly real. Rare mother,
magnanimous mother, forgive your ever unworthy son!

And now, as I collect my strength to write to you I cannot understand why the pen falters in my hand; thoughts,
cloudlike thoughts, come pressing against one another,

each taking its neighbor's place, and some unknown force urges them at one and the same time to pour themselves out before you and holds them back from revealing to you the depths of my devastated soul. I feel the heavy Hand of the Almighty weighing upon me in just punishment. But how dreadful that punishment is! Madman that I was! I attempted to oppose the eternal eloquent desires of the spirit which God Himself inserted in me when He transformed my whole being into thirst—a thirst which the vapid vanities of the world could not quench. He has shown me the road to a foreign clime so that I should nurse there my passions in silence and solitude, amid the hubbub of constant labor and activity, until step by step I rise to the highest level from where I might bestow good by working for the welfare of the world. And I dared reject these divine intentions in order to grovel in this big town among clerks and officials who squander their lives in such a fruitless way. It would be different if a man groveled somewhere where not a single minute of life was lost in futility, where every minute was a storing of rich experience and knowledge; but to fritter away one's entire existence in a place where absolutely nothing looms ahead, where years and years are spent in petty occupations, this would resound in one's soul as a very heavy indictment—this would be death. What happiness is there in attaining at fifty, say, the position of a State Counsellor with wages hardly sufficient for a decent living and without the power to bring mankind a pennyworth of good? The young people of St. Petersburg seem to me very absurd: they keep on shouting that they serve not for the sake of grades, not in order to be rewarded by their superiors—but ask them why they serve at all, and they will not be able to answer; the only apparent reason is that otherwise they would remain at home and twirl their thumbs. Still sillier are those who leave the remote provinces where they own land and where they might have become excellent farmers—instead of the useless people they are. Why, if a person of gentle birth must serve the state, let him serve it in his own manor; but what he does is to dilly-dally in the capital where not only does he not find an office but squanders an incredible amount of money which he gets from home.

In spite of all this I had decided (mainly for your sake) to do my utmost to find a job here; but Providence did not wish it so. Absolutely every attempt I made proved a failure—and strange to say this happened when everything foretold success. People with no capacities whatever and without being sponsored by anyone easily obtained positions which I with the help of protectors could not get. Was it not a clear sign of God's intent, was He not clearly punishing me by these failures in order to make me turn in the right direction? And what did I do? Stubbornly I kept on trying and expecting for months on end some job to turn up. Finally . . . Oh what a dire punishment! Nothing could be more poisonous and cruel! I cannot, I have not the strength to tell you. Mother, dearest mother! You alone are a true friend to me. Will you believe me? Even now, when my thoughts are already elsewhere, even now at the merest recollection, an indescribable oppression crushes my heart. To you alone can I tell it.

As you know, I was endowed with moral firmness—something rare in a young man. Who could have expected any weakness of me? But then I saw her. . . . No, I will not disclose her name. . . . She is too exalted; not I alone —none can attain her. I would have called her an angel but this term does not suit her. She is a goddess all right, but a goddess slightly clothed in human passions. The striking brilliance of her features becomes instantly engraved in one's heart; her eyes instantly pierce one's soul; no human creature can endure her ardent, all-penetrating radiance.

Ah, had you seen me then! 'Tis true I managed to conceal my feelings from the world, but could I conceal them from my own self? An infernal anguish with all possible pangs kept scalding my bosom. In sooth, a cruel state of mind! Methinks if sinners go to hell they suffer less than I did. Nay, 'twas not love . . . or at least never did I know that love could be like that. In a tempest of frenzy and terrific spiritual pain I madly thirsted for the rapture of one glance, yea, only for one glance did I ask. To glance at her only once—this used to be my only desire, and the desire grew stronger and stronger, and was accompanied by a grievous restlessness, the venom of which I cannot express. With horror I looked around and discerned my horrible plight. Absolutely everything in the world had become foreign to me, both life and death were equally unbearable, and my soul could not account for its own phenomena. I saw that I must fly from my own self if I wished to keep alive and have at least the shadow of peace enter my devastated soul. Reverently I recognized the Invisible Hand coming to my assistance and I blessed the path so divinely indicated to me. No, the being that He sent to deprive me of peace and shatter the brittle world I had created was no woman. Had she been a woman, all the strength of her charms could not have produced such terrible, such inexpressible impressions. It was a goddess whom He had created as part of Himself. But for God's sake do not ask me her name. She is too exalted, much too exalted. . . .

Thus my resolution was taken. But how was I to begin? The difficulties of going abroad are so great, the necessary steps so numerous. . . . However, as soon as I set about it I was surprised to see how smoothly everything went. I had even no trouble in obtaining a passport. Finally only one obstacle remained: lack of funds. This was the last stroke, and I had abandoned all hope, when, all of a sudden, I received from you the money which had to be paid to the Custody Board. I immediately went there to find out how long they would be willing to wait with the payment of interest. I learned that the period of grace lasted four months with a monthly penalty of five roubles for every thousand.

In other words they will wait till November. My action is strongheaded and foolhardy, but what else can be done? I have retained all the money due to the Custody Board and now I can firmly assert that I shall never ask you for more. Henceforward my labor and diligence will be my sole reward. As to the payment in full of the sum taken you have the perfect right (which I give you by the warrant of attorney here enclosed) to sell the land which is my due, in part or in toto, to mortgage it, to give it away etc. etc. You may dispose of it in whatever way you desire. At first I wanted to make a deed of purchase or a formal gift but that would have meant spending some three hundred roubles for the necessary paper. Anyway the warrant of attorney is sufficient to make you the lawful and absolute owner of the land.

Do not be sad, good incomparable mother! Such a decisive break was a necessity. This schooling will doubtlessly educate me: I have a bad temper, a corrupt and spoiled nature (this I honestly admit); my idle and sapless existence here would have certainly helped to fix these defects for good. I must alter my nature, must be born and quickened anew, must blossom forth with all the power of my soul amid constant work and activity and if I cannot be happy (nay, I shall never know personal happiness: that divine creature has plucked all peace out of my soul, and gone away far from me), at least I shall devote all my life to the happiness and wellbeing of my brethren.

Let our separation not terrify you, for I am not going far: my road now lies toward Lubeck, a large coastal town in Germany universally known for its commercial relations. It takes four days to get there from Petersburg. I am going by steamer so that it will take me even less. Your letters will travel four days longer, that is all. While this letter is on its way I shall have time to write you from Lubeck letting you know my address. Until then you may address your letters to St. Petersburg, care of His Excellence Nikolai Yakovlevich Prokopovich, at the house of Joachim, Bolshaya Meshchanskaya Street. As to our seeing each other, I am afraid two or three years may elapse before I visit you at Vassilevka. Do not forget to send my man a passport (he cannot stay in the capital without one while I am away); address it as everything else to the care of Prokopovich.

19

And now I embrace the awesome Feet of the Almighty with the humble request and prayer to spare the years of your life so precious and sacred to all of us; to divert anything that might come to cause you grief or displeasure; and to give me strength to deserve a mother's blessing.

P.S. I tender my most heartfelt and inexpressible thanks for the precious information you gave me about Little Russia and beg you not to stop sending me communications of that kind. In the quiet of solitude I am storing up things which I shall not publish before all the details are worked out as I hate to hurry and to do things in a superficial manner. I also want to beg you, dear mother, when you write out personal names and various Ukrainian appellations, to do so as legibly as possible. If my work ever comes out in print it will be in a foreign language, so that basic exactitude is specially important, as otherwise some essential national term might get badly distorted. Excuse me for troubling you even now with such requests, but I take this liberty knowing what pleasure it gives you to heed them. In my turn, I shall describe to you the customs and occupations of the good Germans, the atmosphere of novelty, the strangeness and charm of things seen for the first time, and all matters that may make a strong impression upon me. My gratitude is also due to Father Savva. Tell him I beg him to add his notes to your communications.

You may forward the money straight to the Custody Board. You may wait till November but if would be better if they received it in the middle or in the beginning of October. Do not forget that the monthly penalty is five roubles for every thousand.

HIS DEATH AND HIS YOUTH

If some day you happen to have any spare cash do please send Danilevsky a hundred roubles: I took his fur coat for my voyage and some linen so as not to need anything abroad.

I send my dear sisters Anna and Elisabeth a thousand kisses. For God's sake do your utmost to give Anna a good education. Try to have her master languages and all other useful matters. I prophesy that this wonderful child will turn out to be a unique genius."

I have translated this letter in full because it appears to me like a ball of wool, the diverse threads of which will be found woven into Gogol's later utterings. First of all, whatever his sexual life was (he showed complete indifference towards women insofar as the facts of his riper years show), it is quite obvious that the allusions to the "exalted creature," to the pagan goddess so strangely created by a Christian God, is a purple patch of shameless fiction. Apart from the emphatic declaration of his closest friends who have testified that nothing remotely resembling any romantic disaster ever came young Gogol's way, the style of that part of the letter is so absurdly different from the matter-of-fact rest (with a tell-tale parenthesis inserted in one passage, which blatantly discloses its heterogeneous nature) that one may imagine the author of the letter using for his personal purpose a fragment from some novelette he had been attempting to write in imitation of the inflated fiction of his time. The part about the futility or even sinfulness of striving to become a pen-scratching official in an abstract town instead of cultivating the "real" land given by God to the Russian gentry, foretells the ideas which Gogol later expounded in his *Selected Passages from Let-*

21

ters to Friends; that he himself was quite eager to dispose of that land in any fashion also explains some of their contradictions. The appeal to Providence, or rather the queer way he had (a propensity which his mother shared) of substituting the hand of God for any whim of his own or any chance occurrence in which none but he (and she) could discern the odor of sanctity, is also most suggestive; and it shows how imaginative, humanly imaginative (and thus metaphysically limited) Gogol's religion was, and how little he noticed the Devil he so feared pushing his elbow, while that too fluent pen of his ran on and on; for we observe that immediately after discussing in terms of Providence the evil reality of Russian officialdom, he uses the same Providence for sponsoring an illusion that he had created himself. Realizing that the repulsion he felt for office work would seem a weak reason to his mother, who, like any provincial lady of her day respected a "Collegiate Assessor" less than a "Collegiate Counsellor" (ranks in the Chinese hierarchy of the Russia of her time) he invented something of a more romantic appeal. He also hinted (a hint which as we shall see his mother missed) that the object of his passion was a lady of high birth—perchance the daughter of an "Actual Counsellor of State." That part of the letter which is not directly concerned with fiction is again very typical of Gogol's character. After calmly telling his mother that he took money not belonging to him or at least not intended for his personal use and offering her in exchange property, which he knew she would never make use of, he solemnly swears that he will never ask her for a single penny, and then quite casually asks her for an additional hundred roubles. In the "large commercial town" coming after the divine element there is a bathos which he exploited very artistically in his later writings. Perhaps, the most interesting point in this letter is the notion to which Gogol was to cling so desperately at every critical stage of his literary life that he needed the surroundings of a foreign country —any foreign country—in order to achieve "in the silence of solitude" something that might bring benefit to those "brethren" of his whom he avoided in reality.

On the 13th of July, 1829, wearing his best blue coat with brass buttons, he landed at Lubeck and at once wrote another letter to his mother in which he offered a brand new and equally false explanation of his departure from Petersburg.

"I think I forgot to tell you the main reason for my coming here. During the best part of the spring and summer that I spent in St. Petersburg I had been sick; although eventually I got better, an abundant rash broke out all over my face and hands. According to the doctors this is a consequence of scrofula; my blood is badly contaminated; so they told me to take a blood-cleansing decoction and go through a watering course at Travemuende which is a small town a dozen miles distant from Lubeck."

Apparently he had totally forgotten his romantic invention, but unfortunately his mother had not. Putting two and two together—the mysterious passion and the mysterious rash—the good lady jumped at the conclusion that her son had got entangled with some expensive courtesan and had caught a venereal disease. Gogol was aghast when he received her reply to his two letters. Many times in his life he was to get an unexpected shock after having

spent a good deal of patience, imagination and eloquence
for the purpose of conveying a certain false impression to
his correspondents anent some plan or desire of his own.
Somehow the impression would go wrong, and instead of
receiving an acknowledgement or a bit of constructive
criticism on the same lines and in the same emotional key
that he had used, a jarring shriek of angry protest would
be his only reward. The more pathos he expended, the
more solemn his tone, the deeper his feelings—or at least
the feelings he would express in his most pious and most
irritating style—the stronger and the more unexpected was
the rebuff. He would set out all sails full of the amplest
wind and suddenly scrape his keel on the rocks of what
he treated as a horrible misunderstanding. His reply to
his mother's unexpected attitude towards the illusion that
he had taken considerable pains to stage (its flaw being
the unforeseen combination which its two different parts
formed, for there is nothing more likely to afford the Devil
a weapon than the doubling of plausibility) gives a fore-
taste of his surprise in after years when learning of his
friends' reaction to his ideas about the duties of country
squires or to his desire to give away his literary earnings
in anonymous assistance to needy students instead of
paying his numerous debts to his equally needy friends.
After bitterly protesting against the meaning his mother
had read into his letters, he gave one last excuse for his
leaving Petersburg, and his biographers see in it an allusion to his presumable state of mind after the disaster of
Hanz Kuechelgarten.

"Here is my admission: the proud intentions of youth,
and nothing but they, intentions flowing however from a

pure source—the ardent desire to be useful to mankind—these intentions not being tempered by reason, drove me too far."

The two months which he spent abroad (Lubeck, Travemuende and Hamburg) are difficult to visualize clearly. One biographer has even asserted that he did not go abroad at all that summer, but remained in Petersburg (just as some years later he carefully deceived his mother into thinking he was still in Trieste when he was already back in Moscow). His letters describe the sights of Lubeck in a queer, dreamlike way. It is curious to note that his account of the cathedral clock ("when it is twelve a big marble figure above rings the bell twelve times; the doors above the clock open with a mighty sound; a stately procession of twelve apostles comes out, each figure the size of an ordinary man; they sing and bend their heads as they pass by the statue of our Lord . . .") formed the basic pattern of a nightmare which his mother saw six years later: misfortunes which, she imagined, had befallen Nikolai got mixed up with the clock figures idea, and perhaps this dream, which somehow portended the misery her son would experience in his years of religious mania, was not quite so foolish after all. I find pleasure in following the outlines of these strange shadows lying across those distant lives; and much would I give to find out the name and business of that anonymous American ("a citizen of the American States" as Gogol puts it) who, together with a Swiss couple, an Englishman and a Hindu (transformed into an Indian nabob for the benefit of Gogol's mother) sat down to dinner at that Lubeck inn where a long-nosed young Muscovite busied himself with his food in morose

25

silence. We dream sometimes of perfectly unimportant people, a chance fellow traveler or such like dim person whom we met years ago and never saw again. One may thus imagine a retired business man in the Boston of 1875, casually telling his wife of having dreamt the other night that together with a young Russian or Pole whom he had once met in Germany when he was young himself he was buying a clock and a cloak in a shop of antiques.

5

Gogol returned to Petersburg as unexpectedly as he had left. There was always something bat-like or shadow-like in his flittings from place to place. It was the shadow of Gogol that lived his real life—the life of his books, and in them he was an actor of genius. Would he have made a good actor in the literal sense too? In his aversion towards clerkdom he attempted apparently to go on the stage but evaded or bungled the examination. This was his last attempt to dodge civil service, for towards the end of 1829 we find him launched upon the career of a "chinovnik," his main activity in that capacity being to switch from one branch of the service to another. In the beginning of 1830 he published his first short story, which later on with others was to form the first volume of his Ukrainian tales (*Evenings on a Farm near Dikanka*).

HIS DEATH AND HIS YOUTH

About that time a chapter of a *Historical Novel* (thank goodness never terminated) appeared in *Northern Flowers*, which was a literary magazine edited by Delvig, a poet of the anthological type with leanings towards the classical chill of hexameters. The chapter of the historical novel is signed "OOOO." This quadruplet of zeros is said to be founded on the fact of there being four "o"s in "Nikolai Gogol-Yanovsky." The selection of a void and its multiplication for concealing his identity is very significant on Gogol's part.

In one of his numerous letters to his mother he describes his usual day.

"At nine in the morning I go to the office and remain there until three. I dine at half-past three. Round about five I proceed to the Art Academy class where I study painting—a hobby I simply cannot drop" (he goes on to say that he finds both pleasure and profit in mixing with more or less famous artists). "I cannot help admiring their moods and manners. What men! After one has got to know them one would cling to their company forever. What modesty and what genius! Class work—three times a week—goes on till seven, then I return home and spend the evening with friends of whom I have many. Believe me or not but there are twenty-five of my [Ukrainian] school chums here. . . . At nine in the evening I go for my usual walk. At eleven I come home and make myself tea if I have not had some already. . . . Sometimes I come back from my rambles at midnight or at one o'clock in the morning and still one may see crowds of promeneurs [on the Nevsky and likewise in the suburbs where town folks had their "dachas" (summerhouses)]. As you

27

know, there is no night here: the air is luminous and clear
with the sun alone lacking."

Delvig recommended young Gogol to the poet Zhukovsky, and Zhukovsky recommended him to the literary
critic and University professor Pletniov, who is mainly remembered for Pushkin's dedicating to him *Eugene Onegin.* Pletniov and especially Zhukovsky were to become
Gogol's intimate friends. In mild, pious, mellifluous Zhukovsky he found a mental temperament which faintly
parodied his own—minus, of course, the fierce, almost
medieval passion which Gogol put into his metaphysics.
Zhukovsky, a wonderful translator, who surpassed both
Seidlitz and Schiller in his versions of their poems, and
one of the greatest minor poets that ever was, lived his
life in a kind of golden age of his own, where Providence
ruled in a most gentle and even genteel fashion, and the
incense Zhukovsky dutifully burned, and his honeyed
verse, and the milk of human kindness never curdling in
him, fitted well with Gogol's idea of a pure Russian soul;
and no doubt he experienced no qualms whatever, but
rather on the contrary felt the presence of a pleasant sac-
ramental bond when Zhukovsky expounded certain favorite ideas of his regarding the improvement of the world,
such as for instance the transformation of capital punishment into a religious mystery with the hanging performed
in a closed church-like place to the elevated sound of
hymns, all this invisible to the kneeling crowd, but audi-
torially very beautiful and solemn and inspiring—one of
the reasons Zhukovsky gave for the adoption of this remarkable ritual being that the enclosure, the curtains, the
rich voices of the clergy and choir (drowning any un-

28

seemly sound) would "prevent the condemned man from treating onlookers to a sinful display of swaggering and pluck in the face of death."

Through Pletniov Gogol had the opportunity of replacing the drudgery of civil service by the drudgery of educational work and thus (as a lecturer on history at the Young Ladies' Institute) Gogol's disastrous pedagogic career humbly began. And through the same Pletniov, probably at a party given by the latter in May, 1831, Gogol met Pushkin.

Pushkin had just married and had brought his young wife from Moscow to the capital—instead of locking her up in the darkest closet of a remote country-house as he ought to have done had he known what would come of those ridiculous court-balls and hobnobbing with knavish courtiers (under the supervision of a bland, philandering Tsar, an ignoramus and a cad, whose whole reign was not worth a single foot of Pushkin's verse). His genius was in full swing, but the Russian Renaissance of poetry had passed and a flock of quacks had invaded the courtyards of literature, while pedestrian thought, German "idealism" and the first symptoms of civic minded literary criticism which was to result finally in the ineptitudes of Marxism and Populism, were unanimous in regarding the greatest poet of his time (and perhaps of all time, excepting Shakespeare) as a dusty relic of a past generation or as a representative of the literary "aristocracy"—whatever that is. Earnest readers were yearning for "facts" and "true romance" and "human interest" just as they do now, poor souls.

"I have finished reading *Evenings near Dikanka*," wrote

Pushkin to a friend. "An astounding book! Here is fun for you, authentic fun of the frankest kind without anything maudlin or prim about it. And moreover—what poetry, what delicacy of sentiment in certain passages! All this is so unusual in our literature that I am still unable to get over it. I had been told [Gogol himself imparted the information to Pushkin, and very likely had made it up] that when the author entered the printing house where the *Evenings* were being set, the printers started to chuckle and splutter with mirth; whereupon the overseer explained their hilarity by confessing to the author that they were splitting their sides while setting his book. Molière and Fielding probably would have been glad to make their compositors laugh. I congratulate the reading public on a truly gay book."

Pushkin's praise seems somewhat exaggerated to us now. But it must be remembered that almost nothing of any real worth (except Pushkin's own prose) was being published in the way of Russian fiction. Compared to the trashy imitations of Eighteenth-Century English and French novels which gentle readers were eagerly lapping up in the absence of real spiritual food, Gogol's *Evenings* certainly seemed a revelation. Their charm and their fun have singularly faded since then. Curiously enough, it is on the strength of these *Evenings* (both first and second volumes) that Gogol's fame as a humorist has been based. When a person tells me that Gogol is a "humorist" I know at once that person does not understand much in literature. Had Pushkin lived to read *The Overcoat* and *Dead Souls* he would doubtless have realized that Gogol was something more than a purveyor of "authentic fun." Indeed there is a legend, also it seems of Gogol's making, that when, not long before Pushkin's death, Gogol read to him the first draft of the first chapter of *Dead Souls* Pushkin exclaimed "God, how sad Russia is!"

Couleur locale has been responsible for many hasty appreciations, and local color is *not* a fast color. I have never been able to see eye to eye with people who enjoyed books merely because they were in dialect, or moved in the exotic atmosphere of remote places. The clown who appears in a spangled suit never seems as funny to me as the one who comes in wearing an undertaker's striped pants and a dickey. There is nothing more dull and sickening to my taste than romantic folklore or rollicking yarns about lumberjacks or Yorkshiremen or French villagers or Ukrainian good companions. It is for this reason that the two volumes of the *Evenings* as well as the two volumes of stories entitled *Mirgorod* (containing *Viy, Taras Bulba, Old World Landowners,* etc.) which followed in 1835, leave me completely indifferent. It was however this kind of stuff, the juvenilia of the false humorist Gogol, that teachers in Russian schools crammed down a fellow's throat. The real Gogol dimly transpires in the patchy *Arabesques* (containing *Nevsky Avenue, The Memoirs of a Madman* and *The Portrait*); then bursts into full life with *The Government Inspector, The Overcoat* and *Dead Souls.*

In his *Dikanka* and *Taras Bulba* phase (and how right he was in his riper years to ignore or reject those artificial works of his youth) Gogol was skirting a very dreadful precipice. He almost became a writer of Ukrainian folklore tales and "colorful romances." We must thank fate

31

(and the author's thirst for universal fame) for his not having turned to the Ukrainian dialect as a medium of expression, because then he would have been lost. When I want a good nightmare I imagine Gogol penning in Little Russian dialect volume after volume of *Dikanka* and *Mirgorod* stuff about ghosts haunting the banks of the Dniepr, burlesque Jews and dashing Cossacks.

After a lapse of perhaps twenty-five years I forced myself to reread the *Evenings*—and I remained as unmoved as I had been in the days when my teacher could not understand why *The Terrible Vengeance* did not make my flesh creep or *Shponka and his Aunt* did not make me rock with laughter. But I am aware now that here and there, through that operatic romance and stale farce, something foretelling the real Gogol, something that had been unknown and unintelligible to readers of the eighteen thirties, to the critics of the sixties and to the school teachers of my youth, may be dimly but unmistakably foreseen.

Behold for instance the dream of *Ivan Shponka*—a meek, impotent Ukrainian squire whom his formidable highhanded aunt was trying to bully into marrying a neighbor's big blonde daughter. "He dreamt that he was already married; and everything in his small house was so very unusual and eerie: instead of his bachelor's bed a double one stood in his room; sitting on a chair was his wife. He felt all queer not knowing how to approach her [sitting there on a chair], or what to say, and presently he noticed that she had a goose-face. Happening to turn aside he saw a second wife [the "double" theme of the bed is now beginning to be developed by the special logic of dreams] and she had a goose-face too. He glanced in another direction and lo, there was a third wife standing there; he looked back and saw yet a fourth wife. Dull panic seized him: he ran out into the garden; but it was hot outside and so he took off his hat—and saw a wife sitting in his hat [the dream-conjuror's multiplication trick]. He felt the sweat on his face, groped for his handkerchief—and there was a wife in his pocket; he took the cotton wadding out of his ear—and there sat yet another wife. Then he dreamt that he was skipping on one foot while his aunt looked on and said gravely: 'Yes, you must skip, because now you are a married man.' 'But, auntie,' he began. Too late: his aunt had become a belfry. Then he felt that he was being dragged up that belfry by means of a rope [Freudists will prick up their ears here]. 'Who is dragging me up?'—he moaned in a pitiful voice. 'It is I, your wife, dragging you up, because you are a church-bell.' 'No, I am not a bell, I am Ivan Shponka,' he cried. 'Yes, you are a bell,' said a passer-by, Colonel P. of the Such-and-such Infantry Regiment. Then he dreamt that a wife was not a live person at all, but a kind of woolen fabric and that he was entering the shop of a merchant in Mogilev. 'What cloth would you like?' asked the merchant, and added: 'You had better take some wife, it is the most fashionable stuff, and very solid too—all the gentlemen are making themselves coats of it nowadays,'—and the merchant started to measure and cut the wife. Ivan Shponka took what he was given under his arm and went to a Jewish tailor. 'No,' said the Jew, 'that stuff is no good, nobody makes himself clothes of that stuff nowadays.' Next morning, as soon as he got up, he proceeded at once

33

to open his fortune-telling book [the only book that he ever read] at the end of which a certain virtuous bookseller prompted by a rare sense of kindness and unselfishness had added an abridged Interpretation of Dreams. However, there was absolutely nothing therein that even remotely resembled Shponka's confused dream."

Here, at the close of an otherwise indifferent story we get the first intimation of the weird rhythms which later on made the pattern of *The Overcoat*. The reader will note, I hope, that the most uncanny thing in the passage quoted is not the belfry, not the bell, not the many wives and not even Colonel P., but that horribly casual sentence about the kind and unselfish bookseller.

2. THE GOVERNMENT SPECTER

1

THE HISTORY OF THE PRODUCTION OF GOGOL'S COMEDY *The Government Inspector* on the Russian stage and of the extraordinary stir it created has of course little to do with Gogol, the subject of these notes, but still a few words about those alien matters may be not unnecessary. As it was inevitable that simple minds would see in the play a social satire violently volleyed at the idyllic system of official corruption in Russia, one wonders what hopes the author or anybody else could have had of seeing the play performed. The censors' committee was as blatantly a collection of cringing noodles or pompous asses as all such organizations are, and the mere fact of a writer daring to portray officers of the state otherwise than as abstract figures and symbols of superhuman virtue was a crime that sent shivers down the censors' fat backs. That *The Government Inspector* happened to be the greatest play ever written in Russian (and never surpassed since) was naturally a matter infinitely remote from the committee's mind.

But a miracle happened; a kind of miracle singularly in keeping with the physics of Gogol's upside down world. The Supreme Censor, the One above all, Whose God-like level of being was so lofty as to be hardly mentionable by thick human tongues, the radiant, totalitarian Tsar Himself, in a fit of most unexpected glee commanded the play to be passed and staged.

It is difficult to conjecture what pleased Nicholas I in *The Government Inspector.* The man who a few years before had red-penciled the manuscript of Pushkin's *Boris Godunov* with inane remarks suggesting the turning of that tragedy into a novel on the lines of Walter Scott, and generally was as immune to authentic literature as all rulers are (not excepting Frederic the Great or Napoleon) can hardly be suspected of having seen anything better in Gogol's play than slapstick entertainment. On the other hand a satirical farce (if we imagine for a moment such a delusion in regard to *The Government Inspector*) seems unlikely to have attracted the Tsar's priggish and humorless mind. Given that the man had brains—at least the brains of a politician—it would rather detract from their quantity to suppose that he so much enjoyed the prospect of having his vassals thoroughly shaken up as to be blind to the dangers of having the man in the street join in the imperial mirth. In fact he is reported to have remarked after the first performance: "Everybody has got his due, I most of all"; and if this report is true (which it probably is not) it would seem that the evolutionary link between criticism of corruption under a certain government and

36

criticism of the government itself must have been apparent to the Tsar's mind. We are left to assume that the permission to have the play staged was due to a sudden whim on the Tsar's part, just as the appearance of such a writer as Gogol was a most unexpected impulse on the part of whatever spirit may be held responsible for the development of Russian literature in the beginning of the Nineteenth Century. In signing this permission a despotic ruler was, curiously enough, injecting a most dangerous germ into the blood of Russian writers; dangerous to the idea of monarchy, dangerous to official iniquity, and dangerous—which danger is the most important of the three —to the art of literature; for Gogol's play was misinterpreted by the civic-minded as a social protest and engendered in the fifties and sixties a seething mass of literature denouncing corruption and other social defects and an orgy of literary criticism denying the title of writer to anyone who did not devote his novel or short story to the castigation of district police-officers and moujik-thrashing squires. And ten years later the Tsar had completely forgotten the play and had not the vaguest idea who Gogol was and what he had written.

The first performance of *The Government Inspector* was a vile affair in regard to acting and setting, and Gogol was most bitter in his criticism of the abominable wigs and clownish clothes and gross over-acting that the theater inflicted upon his play. This started the tradition of staging *The Government Inspector* as a burlesque; later to this was added a background suggestive of a *comédie de mœurs*; so that the Twentieth Century inherited a strange concoction of extravagant Gogolian speech and dingy

37

matter-of-fact setting—a state of affairs only solved now and then by the personality of some actor of genius. Strange, it was in the years when the written word was dead in Russia, as it has been now for a quarter of a century, that the Russian producer Meyerhold, in spite of all his distortions and additions, offered a stage version of *The Government Inspector* which conveyed something of the real Gogol.

Only once have I seen the play performed in a foreign language (in English) and it is not a memory I care to evoke. As to the translation of the book, there is little to choose between the Seltzer and Constance Garnett versions. Though totally lacking verbal talent, Garnett has made hers with a certain degree of care and it is thus less irritating than some of the monstrous versions of *The Overcoat* and *Dead Souls*. In a way it may be compared to Guizot's tame translation of *Hamlet*. Of course, nothing has remained of Gogol's style. The English is dry and flat, and always unbearably demure. None but an Irishman should ever try tackling Gogol. Here are some typical instances of inadequate translation (and these may be multiplied): Gogol in his remarks about the two squires, Bobchinsky and Dobchinsky, briefly describes them as both having plump little bellies (or, as he says in another place, "they simply must have protruding tummies—pointed little ones like pregnant women have") which conveys the idea of small and otherwise thin and puny men—and this is most essential for producing the correct impression that Dobchinsky and Bobchinsky must convey. But Constance Garnett translates this as "both rather corpulent," murdering Gogol. I sometimes think that these old Eng-

38

lish "translations" are remarkably similar to the so-called Thousand Pieces Execution which was popular at one time in China. The idea was to cut out from the patient's body one tiny square bit the size of a cough lozenge, say, every five minutes or so until bit by bit (all of them selected with discrimination so as to have the patient live to the nine hundred ninety ninth piece) his whole body was delicately removed.

There are also a number of downright mistakes in that translation such as "clear soup" instead of "oatmeal soup" (which the Charity Commissioner ought to have been giving the sick at the hospital) or—and this is rather funny—a reference to one of the five or six books that the Judge had ever read in his life as "The Book of John the Mason," which sounds like something biblical, when the text really refers to a book of adventures concerning John Mason (or attributed to him), an English diplomatist of the Sixteenth Century and Fellow of All Souls who was employed on the Continent in collecting information for the Tudor sovereigns.

2

The plot of *The Government Inspector* is as unimportant as the plots of all Gogol books.[1] Moreover, in the case of the play, the scheme is the common property of all play-writers: the squeezing of the last drop out of some amusing quid pro quo. It would appear that Pushkin suggested it to Gogol when he told him that while staying at an inn in Nizhni-Novgorod he was mistaken for an important

[1] See page 153 of "Commentaries" for a summary of the plot.

official from the capital; but on the other hand, Gogol, with his head stuffed with old plays ever since his days of amateur theatricals at school (old plays translated into indifferent Russian from three or four languages), might have easily dispensed with Pushkin's prompting. It is strange, the morbid inclination we have to derive satisfaction from the fact (generally false and always irrelevant) that a work of art is traceable to a "true story." Is it because we begin to respect ourselves more when we learn that the writer, just like ourselves, was not clever enough to make up a story himself? Or is something added to the poor strength of our imagination when we know that a tangible fact is at the base of the "fiction" we mysteriously despise? Or taken all in all, have we here that adoration of the truth which makes little children ask the story-teller "Did it really happen?" and prevented old Tolstoy in his hyperethical stage from trespassing upon the rights of the deity and creating, as God creates, perfectly imaginary people? However that may be, some forty years after that first night a certain political émigré was desirous of having Karl Marx (whose *Capital* he was translating in London) know Chernyshevsky, who was a famous radical and conspirator banished to Siberia in the sixties (and one of those critics who vigorously proclaimed the coming of the "Gogolian" era in Russian literature, meaning by this euphemism, which would have horrified Gogol, the duty on the part of novelists to work solely for the improvement of social and political conditions). The political émigré returned secretly to Russia and traveled to the remote Yakoutsk region in the disguise of a Member of the Geographical Society (a nice point, this) in order to kidnap

40

the Siberian prisoner; and his plan was thwarted owing to the fact that more and more people all along his meandering itinerary mistook him for a Government Inspector traveling incognito—exactly as had happened in Gogol's play. This vulgar imitation of artistic fiction on the part of life is somehow more pleasing than the opposite thing.

The epigraph to the play is a Russian proverb which says "Do not chafe at the looking glass if your mug is awry." Gogol, of course, never drew portraits—he used looking glasses and as a writer lived in his own looking glass world. Whether the reader's face was a fright or a beauty did not matter a jot, for not only was the mirror of Gogol's own making and with a special refraction of its own, but also the reader to whom the proverb was addressed belonged to the same Gogolian world of goose-like, pig-like, pie-like, nothing-on-earth-like facial phenomena. Even in his worst writings Gogol was always good at creating his reader, which is the privilege of great writers. Thus we have a circle, a closed family-circle, one might say. It does not open into the world. Treating the play as a social satire (the public view) or as a moral one (Gogol's belated amendment) meant missing the point completely. The characters of *The Government Inspector* whether subject or not to imitation by flesh and blood, were true only in the sense that they were true creatures of Gogol's fancy. Most conscientiously, Russia, that land of eager pupils, started at once living up to these fancies— but that was her business, not Gogol's. In the Russia of Gogol's day bribery flourished as beautifully as it did, and does, anywhere on the Continent—and, on the other hand, there doubtless existed far more disgusting scoundrels in any Russian town of Gogol's time than the good-natured rogues of *The Government Inspector*. I have a lasting grudge against those who like their fiction to be educational or uplifting, or national, or as healthy as maple syrup and olive oil, so that is why I keep harping on this rather futile side of *The Government Inspector* question.

3

The play begins with a blinding flash of lightning and ends in a thunderclap. In fact it is wholly placed in the tense gap between the flash and the crash. There is no so-called "exposition." Thunderbolts do not lose time explaining meteorological conditions. The whole world is one ozone-blue shiver and we are in the middle of it. The only stage tradition of his time that Gogol retained was the soliloquy, but then people do talk to themselves aloud during the nervous hush before a storm while waiting for the bang to come. The characters are nightmare people in one of those dreams when you think you have waked up while all you have done is to enter the most dreadful (most dreadful in its sham reality) region of dreams. Gogol has a peculiar manner of letting "secondary" dream characters pop out at every turn of the play (or novel, or story), to flaunt for a second their life-like existence (as that Colonel P. who passed by in *Shponka's Dream* or many a creature in *Dead Souls*). In *The Government Inspector* this manner is apparent from the start in the weird private letter which the Town-Mayor Skvoznik-Dmukhanovsky reads aloud to his subordinates—School Inspector Khlopov, Judge Lyapkin-Tyapkin (Mr. Slap-
42

Dash), Charity Commissioner Zemlyanika, (Mr. Strawberry—an overripe brown strawberry wounded by the lip of a frog) and so forth. Note the nightmare names so different from, say, the sleek "Hollywood Russian" pseudonyms Vronsky, Oblonsky, Bolkonsky etc. used by Tolstoy. (The names Gogol invents are really nicknames which we surprise in the very act of turning into family names—and a metamorphosis is a thing always exciting to watch.) After reading the important part of the letter referring to the impending arrival of a governmental inspector from Petersburg the Mayor automatically continues to read aloud and his mumbling engenders remarkable secondary beings that struggle to get into the front row.

". . . my sister Anna Kyrillovna and her husband have come to stay with us; Ivan Kyrillovich [apparently a brother, judging by the patronymic] has grown very fat and keeps playing the violin."

The beauty of the thing is that these secondary characters will not appear on the stage later on. We all know those casual allusions at the beginning of Act I to Aunt So-and-so or to the Stranger met on the train. We all know that the "by the way" which introduces these people really means that the Stranger with the Australian accent or the Uncle with the comical hobby would have never been mentioned if they were not to breeze in a moment later. Indeed the "by the way" is generally a sure indication, the masonic sign of conventional literature, that the person alluded to will turn out to be the main character of the play. We all know that trite trick, that coy spirit haunting first acts in Scribia as well as on Broadway. A famous

43

playwright has said (probably in a testy reply to a bore wishing to know the secrets of the craft) that if in the first act a shot gun hangs on the wall, it must go off in the last act. But Gogol's guns hang in midair and do not go off—in fact the charm of his allusions is exactly that nothing whatever comes of them.

In giving his instructions to his subordinates in view of preparing and repairing things for the arrival of the Government Inspector, the Mayor refers to the Judge's clerk.

". . . a knowing fellow, I daresay, but he has such a smell coming from him—as if he had just emerged from a vodka distillery. . . . I meant to mention it to you [to the Judge] long ago but something or other kept putting it out of my head. Remedies may be found if, as he says, it is his natural odor: you might suggest to him a diet of onions or garlic, or something of that kind. In a case like this Christian Ivanovich [the silent District Doctor of German extraction] might help by supplying this or that drug."

To which the Judge retorts:

"No, it is a thing impossible to dislodge: he tells me that his wet nurse dropped him when he was a baby and that there has been a slight smell of vodka hanging about him ever since."

"Well [says the Mayor] I just wanted to draw your attention to it, that is all." And he turns to another official.

We shall never hear about that unfortunate clerk again, but there he is, alive, a whimsical, smelly creature of that "injured" kind over which Gogol smacked his lips.

Other secondary beings have no time to come out in full attire, so impatient are they to jump into the play between two sentences. The Mayor is now drawing the attention of the School Inspector to his assistants:

"One of them, for instance, the one with the fat face . . . can't think of his name . . . well, every time he begins his class, he simply must make a grimace, like this [shows how] and then he starts to massage his chin from under his cravat. Of course if he makes faces only at the boys, it does not much matter—it may be even necessary in his department for all I know of those things; but consider what might happen if he did it in front of a visitor—that would be really dreadful: His Excellency the Government Inspector or anybody else might think it was meant for him. Goodness only knows what consequences that might have."

"What on earth am I to do with him, pray? [replies the School Inspector]. I have spoken to him several times already. Only the other day when our Marshal of Nobility was about to enter the classroom he went into such facial contortions as I have never yet seen. He did not mean anything, bless his kind heart, but *I* got a wigging: suggesting revolutionary ideas to youth, that's what they said."

Immediately afterwards another homunculus appears [rather like the little firm heads of witch doctors bursting out of the body of an African explorer in a famous short story]. The Mayor refers to the history teacher:

"He is a scholar, no doubt, and has acquired loads of learning, but there—he lectures with such vehemence that he loses all self-control. I happened to hear him once: so long as he was talking about the Assyrians and the Babylonians it was—well, one could stand it; but when

45

he got to Alexander the Great, then—no, I simply can't describe his state. Lord, I thought the house was on fire! He dashed out of his desk and banged a chair against the floor with all his might! Alexander the Great was a hero, we all know that, but is this a reason to break chairs? It is wasting Government property."

"Ah yes, he is vehement [admits the School Inspector with a sigh] I have mentioned it to him several times. He answers: whether you like it or not, I can't help forfeiting my own life in the cause of learning."

The Postmaster, to whom the Mayor talks next, asking him to unseal and read the letters that pass through his office (which the good man had been doing for his own pleasure for years), is instrumental in letting out another homunculus.

"It's a great pity [he says to the Mayor] that you don't read those letters yourself: they contain some admirable passages. The other day for instance a lieutenant was writing to a friend and describing a ball he had been to—in a most waggish style. . . . Oh, very, very nice: 'My life, dear friend,' he wrote, 'floats in empyrean bliss: lots of young ladies, band playing, banner galloping . . .'—all of it written with great, great feeling."

Two quarrelsome country squires are mentioned next by the Judge, Cheptovich and Varkhovinsky, neighbors, who have taken proceedings against each other which will probably last all their lives (while the Judge merrily courses hares on the lands of both). Then as Dobchinsky and Bobchinsky make their dramatic appearance with the news that they have discovered the Government Inspector living incognito at the local inn, Gogol parodies his own

46

fantastic meandering way (with gushes of seemingly irrelevant details) of telling a story: all the personal friends
of Bobchinsky come bobbing up as the latter launches
upon the report of his and Dobchinsky's sensational dis-
covery: "So I ran to see Korobkin [Mr. Box] and not finding Korobkin at home [Jack-in-the-box had left it], I
called on Rastakovsky [Mr. Blankety-Blank], and not
finding Rastakovsky at home . . . [of all the homunculi
only these two will appear as visitors at the end of the
last act by special request of the stage management]."
At the inn where Bobchinsky and Dobchinsky see the
person whom they wrongly suspect to be the Government
Inspector they interview the inn-keeper Vlass—and here
—among the gasps and splutters of Bobchinsky's feverish
speech (trying to tell it all before his double, Dobchinsky,
can interrupt him) we obtain this lovely detailed information concerning Vlass (for in Gogol's world the more a
person hurries the more he loiters on the way):

". . . and so Dobchinsky beckoned with his finger and
called the inn-keeper—you know, the inn-keeper Vlass—
his wife has borne him a child three weeks ago—such a
smart little beggar—will keep an inn just like his father
does. . . ."

Note how the newborn Anonymous Vlassovich manages to grow up and live a whole life in the space of a
second. Bobchinsky's panting speech seems to provoke an
intense fermentation in the backstage world where those
homunculi breed.

There are some more to come. The room where Khlestakov—the sham Government Inspector—dwells is identi-
fied by the fact that some officers who had also chanced to

47

pass through that town some time before had a fight there over cards. One of the Mayor's men, the policeman Prokhorov, is alluded to in the following way.

The Mayor, in blustering haste to the policeman Svistunov: "Where are the others? . . . Dear me, I had ordered Prokhorov to be here, too. Where is Prokhorov?"

The Policeman: "Prokhorov is at the police station, but he cannot be put to any good use."

The Mayor: "How's that?"

The Policeman: "Well, just as I say: he was brought in this morning in a carriage dead drunk. Two buckets of water have been poured over him already, but he has not come round yet."

"But how on earth did you let him get into such a state?" the Mayor asks a moment later, and the Police Officer (incidentally called Ukhovyortov—a name which contains the idea of "viciously hitting people on the ear" all in one word) replies: "The Lord knows. There was a brawl in the suburb yesterday—he went there to settle matters and came back drunk."

After this orgy of secondary characters surging at the close of the first act there is a certain lull in the second which introduces Khlestakov. True, a gambling infantry captain, who was great at piling up tricks, appears to the echoes of cheerful card-slapping as Khlestakov recalls the money he lost to him in the town of Pensa; but otherwise the active, ardent Khlestakov theme is too vigorous in this act (with the Mayor visiting him at the inn) to suffer any intruders. They come creeping back in the third act: Zemlyanika's daughter, we learn, wears a blue frock—and so she floats by in between the speeches, a pink and blue provincial maiden.

When upon his arrival at the Mayor's house Khlestakov, in the most famous scene of the Russian stage, starts showing off for the benefit of the ladies, the secondary characters that come tumbling out of his speech (for at last they had been set rolling by Khlestakov's natural garrulousness and the Mayor's wine) are of another race, so to speak, than those we have already met. They are of a lighter, almost transparent texture in keeping with Khlestakov's own iridescent temperament—phantoms in the guise of civil servants, gleeful imps coming to the assistance of the versatile devil ventriloquizing through Khlestakov. Dobchinsky's children, Vanya, Lisanka, or the inn-keeper's boy existed somewhere or other, but these do not exist at all, as such. The allusions have become delusions. But because of the crescendo of lies on Khlestakov's part the driving force of these metaphysical creatures is more felt in its reaction upon the course of the play than were the idyllic gambols of the little people in the background of Act I.

"Ah, Petersburg!" exclaims Khlestakov. "That is what I call life! Perhaps you think I am just a copying clerk? [which he was]. No, Sir, the head of my section is right chummy with me. Has a way, you know, of slapping me on the shoulder and saying: 'Come and have dinner with me, old chap.' I only look in at the office for a couple of minutes, just to tell them: 'Do this, do that.' And then the copying clerk, old rat, goes with his pen—trrk, trrk, scraping and scribbling away. [In long drawn accents] It was

49

even suggested that I be made a Collegiate Assessor. [Again trippingly] But thought I to myself, what's the use? And there is the office boy [these are bearded men in Russia] running up the stairs after me with a brush— 'Allow me, Sir,' he says, 'I'll just give a bit of shining to your shoes.'" Much later we learn that the office "boy's" name was Mikhey, and that he drank like a fish.

Further on, when, according to Khlestakov, soldiers rushed out of the guardhouse as he passed and gave the grand salute: "Their officer whom I knew very well said to me afterwards: 'Well, well, old boy, I am damned if we did not take you for the Commander-in-Chief!'"

When he starts talking of his Bohemian and literary connections, there even appears a goblin impersonating Pushkin: "I hobnob with Pushkin. Many a time have I said to him: 'Well, old Push, how are things going?'—'As usual, my dear fellow,' he says, 'very much as usual.' Quite a character!"

Then other bigwigs come jostling and buzzing and tumbling over each other as Khlestakov rushes on in an ecstasy of invention: Cabinet Ministers, Ambassadors, Counts, Princes, Generals, the Tsar's Advisors, a shadow of the Tsar himself, and "Messengers, messengers, messengers, thirty-five thousand messengers," spermatozoids of the brain—and then suddenly in a drunken hiccup they all fade; but not before a real allusion (at least real in the same sense as the little people of Act I were "real"), the ghost of needy clerk Khlestakov's slatternly cook Mavroosha peeps out for a dreadful instant through a chink of Khlestakov's speech in the midst of all those golden ghosts and dream ambassadors—to help him out of his skimpy overcoat (that carrick, to be exact, which later on Gogol was to immortalize as the attribute of a transcendental "chinovnik").

In the next act, when one by one the nervous officials present their respects to Khlestakov, who borrows money from each (they think that they are bribing him) we learn the names of Zemlyanika's children—Nicholas, Ivan, Elizabeth, Mary and Perepetuya: it was probably gentle Perepetuya who wore the pale blue frock. Of Dobchinsky's three children, two have been mentioned already by the Mayor's wife as being her godchildren. They and the eldest boy are uncommonly like the Judge who visits Mrs. Dobchinsky every time her poor little husband is away. The eldest boy was born before Dobchinsky married that wayward lady. Dobchinsky says to Khlestakov: "I make bold to ask your assistance in regard to a most delicate circumstance. . . . My eldest son, Sir, was born before I was married. . . . Oh, it is only a manner of speaking. I engendered him exactly as though in lawful wedlock, and made it perfectly right afterwards by sealing the bonds, Sir, of legitimate matrimony, Sir. Well, now I want him to be, in a manner of speaking, altogether my legitimate son, Sir, and to be called the same as I: Dobchinsky, Sir." (The French "sauf votre respect," though much too long, would perhaps better render the meaning of the humble little hiss—an abbreviation of "Soodar"—"Sir," which Dobchinsky adds to this or that word at the fall of his sentences.)

"I would not have troubled you," he goes on, "but I feel sorry for him, seeing his many gifts. The little fellow, you see, is something quite special—promises a lot: he can recite verses and such like things by heart, and whenever

he happens to come across a penknife he makes a wee
little carriage—as clever as a conjuror, Sir."

One more character appears in the background of the
act: it is when Khlestakov decides to write about those
weird provincial officials to his friend Tryapichkin (Mr.
Ragman) who is a sordid little journalist with mercenary
and pamphleteering inclinations, a rascal with a knack of
making laughing stocks of those he chooses to chastise in
his cheap but vicious articles. For one instant he winks
and leers over Khlestakov's shoulder. He is the last to
appear—no, not quite the last, for the ultimate phantom
will be the gigantic shadow of the real Government Inspector.

This secondary world, bursting as it were through the
background of the play, is Gogol's true kingdom. It is remarkable that these sisters and husbands and children,
eccentric school teachers, vodka-bewitched clerks and
policemen, country squires quarreling for fifty years over
the position of a fence, romantic officers who cheat at
cards, wax sentimental over provincial balls and take a
ghost for the Commander-in-Chief, these copying clerks
and fantastic messengers—all these creatures whose lively
motion constitutes the very material of the play, not only
do not interfere with what theatrical managers call "action" but apparently assist the play to be eminently play-
able.

4

Not only live creatures swarm in that irrational background but numerous objects are made to play a part as
important as that of the characters: the hatbox which the

THE GOVERNMENT SPECTER

Mayor places upon his head instead of his hat when stamping out in official splendor and absent-minded haste to meet a threatening phantom, is a Gogolian symbol of the sham world where hats are heads, hatboxes hats, and braided collars the backbones of men. The hurried note which the Mayor sends from the inn to his wife telling her of the exalted guest whom she must get ready to receive gets mixed up with Khlestakov's hotel bill, owing to the Mayor having used the first scrap of paper that came to hand: "I hasten to tell you, my dearest, that I was in a most sorry plight at first; but thanks to my trusting in the mercy of God 2 salted cucumbers extra and ½ a portion of caviare, 1 rouble 25 kopeks." This confusion is again a piece of sound logic within Gogol's world, where the name of a fish is an outburst of divine music to the ears of gourmets, and cucumbers are metaphysical beings at least as potent as a provincial town mayor's private deity. These cucumbers breed in Khlestakov's eloquent description of his ideal of noble living: "On the table for instance there is a watermelon [which is but a sublimated cucumber] —not an ordinary watermelon but one that costs 700 roubles." The watery soup "with feathers or something floating in it" [instead of golden eyelets of shimmering fat] which Khlestakov has to be content with at the inn is transformed in the speech referring to his life in the capital into a *potage* that comes in a pan "straight from Paris by steamer,"—the smoke of that imaginary steamer being as it were the heavenly exhalation of that imaginary soup. When Khlestakov is being made comfortable in his carriage the Mayor has a blue Persian rug brought from the store room (which is crammed with the compulsory

offerings of his bearded subjects—the town merchants);
Khlestakov's valet adds to this a padding of hay—and the
rug is transformed into a magic carpet on which Khlestakov makes his volatile exit backstage to the silvery
sound of the horse-bells and to the coachman's lyrical ad-
monition to his magical steeds: "Hey you, my winged
ones!" ("Hey vy, zalyotnye!" which literally means, "the
ones that fly far"): Russian coachmen are apt to invent
fond names for their horses—and Gogol, it may be assumed (for the benefit of those who like to know the personal experiences of writers) was to acquire a good deal
of viatic lore during the endless peregrinations of his later
years; and this gust of poetry, in which Khlestakov—the
dreamy infantile swindler—fades out seems to blow open
the gates for Gogol's own departure from the Russia he
had invented towards distant hazy climes where number-
less German watering towns, Italian ruins, Parisian restau-
rants and Palestine's shrines were to get mixed up in
much the same way as Providence and a couple of cucumbers did in the distracted Mayor's letter.

5

It is amusing to recall that this dream play, this "Government Specter," was treated as a skit on actual conditions
in Russia. It is still more amusing to think that Gogol in
his first dismal effort to check those dangerous revolutionary allusions to his play pointed out that there was at least
one positive character in it: Laughter. The truth is that
the play is not a "comedy" at all, just as Shakespeare's
dream-plays *Hamlet* or *Lear* cannot be called "tragedies."

THE GOVERNMENT SPECTER

A bad play is more apt to be good comedy or good tragedy than the incredibly complicated creations of such men as Shakespeare or Gogol. In this sense Molière's stuff (for what it is worth) is "comedy" i. e. something as readily assimilated as a hot dog at a football game, something of one dimension and absolutely devoid of the huge, seething, prodigiously poetic background that makes true drama. And in the same sense O'Neill's *Mourning Becomes Electra* (for what *that* is worth) is, I suppose, a "tragedy."

Gogol's play is poetry in action, and by poetry I mean the mysteries of the irrational as perceived through rational words. True poetry of that kind provokes—not laughter and not tears—but a radiant smile of perfect satisfaction, a purr of beatitude—and a writer may well be proud of himself if he can make his readers, or more exactly some of his readers, smile and purr that way.

Khlestakov's very name is a stroke of genius, for it conveys to the Russian reader an effect of lightness and rashness, a prattling tongue, the swish of a slim walking cane, the slapping sound of playing cards, the braggadocio of a nincompoop and the dashing ways of a lady-killer (minus the capacity for completing this or any other action). He flutters through the play as indifferent to a full comprehension of the stir he creates, as he is eager to grab the benefits that luck is offering him. He is a gentle soul, a dreamer in his own way, and a certain sham charm hangs about him, the grace of a petit-maître that affords the ladies a refined pleasure as being in contrast with the boorish ways of the burly town worthies. He is utterly and deliciously vulgar, and the ladies are vulgar, and the worthies are vulgar—in fact the whole play is (somewhat like *Madame Bovary*) composed by blending in a special way different aspects of vulgarity so that the prodigious artistic merit of the final result is due (as with all master-pieces) not to *what* is said but to *how* it is said—to the dazzling combinations of drab parts. As in the scaling of insects the wonderful color effect may be due not to the pigment of the scales but to their position and refractive power, so Gogol's genius deals not in the intrinsic qualities of computable chemical matter (the "real life" of literary critics) but in the mimetic capacities of the physical phe-nomena produced by almost intangible particles of re-created life. I have employed the term "vulgarity" for lack of a more precise one; so Pushkin in *Eugene Onegin* inserted the English word "vulgar" with apologies for not finding in the Russian language its exact counterpart.

6

The charges directed against *The Government Inspec-tor* by resentful people who saw in it an insidious attack against Russian officialdom had a disastrous effect upon Gogol. It may be said to have been the starting point of the persecution mania that in various forms afflicted him to the very end of his life. The position was rather curious: fame, in its most sensational form, had come to him; the Court was applauding his play with almost vicious glee; the stuffed shirts of high officialdom were losing their stuffing as they moved uneasily in their orchestra seats; disreputable critics were discharging stale venom; such critics whose opinion was worth something were lauding Gogol to the stars for what they thought was a great satire;

the popular playwright Kukolnik shrugged his shoulders and said the play was nothing but a silly farce; young people repeated with gusto its best jokes and discovered Khlestakovs and Skvosnik-Dmukhanovskys among their acquaintances. Another man would have reveled in this atmosphere of praise and scandal. Pushkin would have merely shown his gleaming Negro teeth in a good-natured laugh—and turned to the unfinished manuscript of his current masterpiece. Gogol did what he had done after the *Kuechelgarten* fiasco: he fled, or rather slithered, to foreign lands.

He did something else, too. In fact he did the worst thing that a writer could do under the circumstances: he started explaining in print such points of his play as his critics had either missed or directed against him. Gogol, being Gogol and living in a looking-glass world, had a knack of thoroughly planning his works *after* he had written and published them. This system he applied to *The Government Inspector*. He appended a kind of epilogue to it in which he explained that the real Government Inspector who looms at the end of the last act is the Conscience of Man. And that the other characters are the Passions in our Souls. In other words one was supposed to believe that these Passions were symbolized by grotesque and corrupt provincial officials and that the higher Conscience was symbolized by the Government. This explanation has the same depressing effect as his later considerations of related subjects have—unless we can believe that he was pulling his reader's leg—or his own. Viewed as a plain statement we have here the incredible fact of a writer totally misunderstanding and distorting the sense of his

57

own work. He did the same to *Dead Souls*, as will be seen.

He was a strange sick creature—and I am not sure that his explanation of *The Government Inspector* is not the kind of deceit that is practiced by madmen. It is difficult to accept the notion that what distressed him so dreadfully about the reception of his play was his failure to be recognized as a prophet, a teacher, a lover of mankind (giving mankind a warning for its own good). There is not a speck of didacticism in the play and it is inconceivable that the author could be unaware of this; but as I say, he was given to dreaming things into his books long after they had been written. On the other hand the kind of lesson which critics—quite wrongly—discerned in the play was a social and almost revolutionary one which was highly distasteful to Gogol. He may have been apprehensive of the Court suddenly changing its august and fickle mind owing to the too violent praise in radical circles and to the too violent blame in reactionary ones—and thus cutting short the performances and profits (and a future pension maybe). He may have seen his literary career in Russia hampered for years to come by vigilant censors. He may too have been shocked and hurt by the fact that people whom he respected as good Christians (though the "good Christian" theme in its full form was to appear somewhat later) and good officials (which was to become synonymous with the first) were grieved and revolted by what they termed a "coarse and trivial farce." But what seems to have tormented him above all was the knowledge of being talked about by thousands of people and not being able to hear, let alone control, the talk. The buzz that reached him was ominous and monstrous because it was a buzz.

THE GOVERNMENT SPECTER

The pats he received on his back seemed to him to imply ironic sneers directed at people whom he respected, so that these sneers were also directed at himself. The interest that perfect strangers showed in regard to him seemed alive with dark stratagems and incalculable dangers (beautiful word, stratagem—a treasure in a cave). I shall have occasion to speak in quite a different book of a lunatic who constantly felt that all the parts of the landscape and movements of inanimate objects were a complex code of allusion to his own being, so that the whole universe seemed to him to be conversing about him by means of signs. Something of that sinister and almost cosmic dumbshow can be inferred from the morbid view Gogol took of his sudden celebrity. He fancied a hostile Russia creeping and whispering all around him and trying to destroy him both by blaming and praising his play. In June, 1836, he left for Western Europe.

It is said that on the eve of his departure Pushkin, whom he was never to see again, visited him and spent all night rummaging together with him among his manuscripts and reading the beginning of *Dead Souls*, a first draft of which had already been made by Gogol about that time. The picture is pleasing—too pleasing perhaps to be true. For some reason or other (possibly from a morbid dislike of any responsibility) Gogol in after years was most anxious to have people believe that all he had written before 1837, that is, before Pushkin's death, had been directly due to the latter's suggestion and influence. As Gogol's art was as far removed from that of Pushkin as could be and as moreover Pushkin had other problems to tackle than guiding the pen of a literary acquaintance, the information so read-

59

ily supplied by Gogol himself is hardly worth serious consideration. The lone candle lighting up the midnight scene may go out without any qualms on our part. What is far more likely is that Gogol stole abroad without bidding farewell to any of his friends. We know from a letter of his that he did not even say good-bye to Zhukovsky with whom he was on much more intimate terms than with Pushkin.

3. OUR MR. CHICHIKOV

1

THE OLD TRANSLATIONS OF "DEAD SOULS" [1] INTO ENGLISH ARE absolutely worthless and should be expelled from all public and university libraries. While I was writing the notes which form this book, and after I had taken the trouble of translating myself such passages as I required, The Readers' Club in New York published a completely new translation of *Dead Souls*, made by B. G. Guerney. It is an extraordinarily fine piece of work. The edition is marred however by two things: a ridiculous foreword contributed by one of the members of the Club's editorial committee and the alteration of the authentic title to *Chichikov's Journeys, or Homelife in Old Russia*. This is especially distressing if we remember that the title *Chichikov's Journeys* was enforced by the Tsar's censorship for the first

[1] See page 159 in the "Chronology" for a summary of the plot of *Dead Souls*.

Russian edition—because: "the Church tells us that souls are immortal and so cannot be called 'dead.'" In the present case a similar change has apparently been prompted by the fear of suggesting gloomy ideas to rosy-cheeked comic strip fans. The subtitle *Homelife in Old Russia* is also unfortunate as it is based on that of a spurious edition: *Homelife in Russia by a Russian Noble, revised by the editor of Revelations of Siberia*, London, Hurst and Blackett, Publishers, successors to Henry Colburn, 13 Great Marlborough Street, 1854, with the remarkable notice "This Work is Copyright and the Publishers reserve to themselves the Right of Translation" and a foreword containing the following no less remarkable passages:

"The Work is written by a Russian nobleman, who offered the Ms. in English to the publishers, and the editor's task has been confined to altering such verbal errors as might be expected, when we bear in mind that the Author has written in a language which is not his own. . . . It gives us an insight into the internal circumstances and relations of Russian society. . . . The Author affirms that the story is true, and that the main facts are well known in Russia.

". . . In conclusion we may regret that we are not at liberty to mention the Author's name—not that the work itself requires any further verification, for its genuineness is avouched by almost every line—but the truth is, that the writer is still anxious to return to his native country, and is perfectly well aware that the avowal of his handiwork and such a display of his satirical power, will not serve as a special recommendation except possibly as a passport to the innermost regions of the Siberian wilds."

62

OUR MR. CHICHIKOV

One would very much like to know the identity of that Russian nobleman who translated (with various Victorian adornments added by his Editor) *Dead Souls* and sold his stuff to an English firm that apparently thought they were publishing authentic memoirs "which throw light upon the domestic life of our ancient allies and present foes." Was that nobleman called Khlestakov? Was it Chichikov himself? In a way Gogol's book has had a most Gogolian fate.

2

The Russian language is able to express by means of one pitiless word the idea of a certain widespread defect for which the other three European languages I happen to know possess no special term. The absence of a particular expression in the vocabulary of a nation does not necessarily coincide with the absence of the corresponding notion but it certainly impairs the fullness and readiness of the latter's perception. Various aspects of the idea which Russians concisely express by the term *poshlost* (the stress-accent is on the puff-ball of the first syllable, and the final "t" has a moist softness that is hardly equaled by the French "t" in such words as "restiez" or "émoustillant") are split among several English words and thus do not form a definite whole. On second thought, I find it preferable to transcribe that fat brute of a word thus: *poshlust*—which renders in a somewhat more adequate manner the dull sound of the second, neutral "o." Inversely the first "o" is as big as the plop of an elephant falling into a muddy pond and as round as the bosom of a bathing beauty on a German picture postcard.

English words expressing several, although by no means all aspects of *poshlust* are for instance: "cheap, sham, common, smutty, pink-and-blue, high falutin', in bad taste." My little assistant, *Roget's Thesaurus,* (which incidentally lists "rats, mice" under "Insects"—see page 21 of Revised Edition) supplies me moreover with "inferior, sorry, trashy, scurvy, tawdry, gimcrack" and others under "cheapness." All these however suggest merely certain false values for the detection of which no particular shrewdness is required. In fact they tend, these words, to supply an obvious classification of values at a given period of human history; but what Russians call *poshlust* is beautifully timeless and so cleverly painted all over with protective tints that its presence (in a book, in a soul, in an institution, in a thousand other places) often escapes detection.

Ever since Russia began to think, and up to the time that her mind went blank under the influence of the extraordinary regime she has been enduring for these last twenty-five years, educated, sensitive and free-minded Russians were acutely aware of the furtive and clammy touch of *poshlust*. Among the nations with which we came into contact, Germany had always seemed to us a country where *poshlust*, instead of being mocked, was one of the essential parts of the national spirit, habits, traditions and general atmosphere, although at the same time well-meaning Russian intellectuals of a more romantic type readily, too readily, adopted the legend of the greatness of German philosophy and literature; for it takes a super-Russian to admit that there is a dreadful streak of *poshlust* running through Goethe's *Faust*.

64

OUR MR. CHICHIKOV

To exaggerate the worthlessness of a country at the awkward moment when one is at war with it—and would like to see it destroyed to the last beer-mug and last forget-me-not,—means walking dangerously close to that abyss of *poshlust* which yawns so universally at times of revolution or war. But if what one demurely murmurs is but a mild pre-war truth, even with something old-fashioned about it, the abyss is perhaps avoidable. Thus, a hundred years ago, while civic-minded publicists in St. Petersburg were mixing heady cocktails of Hegel and Schlegel (with a dash of Feuerbach), Gogol, in a chance story he told, expressed the immortal spirit of *poshlust* pervading the German nation and expressed it with all the vigor of his genius.

The conversation around him had turned upon the subject of Germany, and after listening awhile, Gogol said: "Yes, generally speaking the average German is not too pleasant a creature, but it is impossible to imagine anything more unpleasant than a German Lothario, a German who tries to be winsome. . . . One day in Germany I happened to run across such a gallant. The dwelling place of the maiden whom he had long been courting without success stood on the bank of some lake or other, and there she would be every evening sitting on her balcony and doing two things at once: knitting a stocking and enjoying the view. My German gallant being sick of the futility of his pursuit finally devised an unfailing means whereby to conquer the heart of his cruel Gretchen. Every evening he would take off his clothes, plunge into the lake and, as he swam there, right under the eyes of his beloved, he would keep embracing a couple of swans which had

65

been specially prepared by him for that purpose. I do not quite know what those swans were supposed to symbolize, but I do know that for several evenings on end he did nothing but float about and assume pretty postures with his birds under that precious balcony. Perhaps he fancied there was something poetically antique and mythological in such frolics, but whatever notion he had, the result proved favorable to his intentions: the lady's heart was conquered just as he thought it would be, and soon they were happily married."

Here you have *poshlust* in its ideal form, and it is clear that the terms trivial, trashy, smug and so on do not cover the aspect it takes in this epic of the blond swimmer and the two swans he fondled. Neither is it necessary to travel so far both in space and time to obtain good examples. Open the first magazine at hand and you are sure to find something of the following kind: a radio set (or a car, or a refrigerator, or table silver—anything will do) has just come to the family: mother clasps her hands in dazed delight, the children crowd around, all agog, Junior and the dog strain up to the edge of the table where the Idol is enthroned; even Grandma of the beaming wrinkles peeps out somewhere in the background (forgetful, we presume, of the terrific row she has had that very morning with her daughter-in-law); and somewhat apart, his thumbs gleefully inserted in the armpits of his waistcoat, legs a-straddle and eyes a-twinkle, stands triumphant Pop, the Proud Donor.

The rich *poshlust* emanating from advertisements of this kind is due not to their exaggerating (or inventing) the glory of this or that serviceable article but to suggesting that the acme of human happiness is purchasable and that its purchase somehow ennobles the purchaser. Of course, the world they create is pretty harmless in itself because everybody knows that it is made up by the seller with the understanding that the buyer will join in the make-believe. The amusing part is not that it is a world where nothing spiritual remains except the ecstatic smiles of people serving or eating celestial cereals or a world where the game of the senses is played according to bourgeois rules ("bourgeois" in the Flaubertian, *not* in the Marxist sense) but that it is a kind of satellite shadow world in the actual existence of which neither sellers nor buyers really believe in their heart of hearts—especially in this wise quiet country.

If a commercial artist wishes to depict a nice little boy he will grace him with freckles (which incidentally assume a horrible rash-like aspect in the humbler funnies). Here *poshlust* is directly connected with a forgotten convention of a faintly racial type. Kind people send our lonely soldiers silk hosed dummy legs modeled on those of Hollywood lovelies and stuffed with candies and safety razor blades—at least I have seen a picture of a person preparing such a leg in a certain periodical which is a world-famous purveyor of *poshlust*. Propaganda (which could not exist without a generous supply of and demand for *poshlust*) fills booklets with lovely Kolkhos maidens and windswept clouds. I select my examples hurriedly and at random—the "Encyclopédie des Idées Reçues" which Flaubert dreamt of writing one day was a more ambitious work.

Literature is one of its best breeding places and by

67

poshlust-literature I do not mean the kind of thing which is termed "pulp" or which in England used to go under the name of "penny dreadfuls" and in Russia under that of "yellow literature." Obvious trash, curiously enough, contains sometimes a wholesome ingredient, readily appreciated by children and simple souls. Superman is undoubtable *poshlust*, but it is *poshlust* in such a mild, unpretentious form that it is not worth while talking about; and the fairy tales of yore contained, for that matter, as much trivial sentiment and naive vulgarity as these yarns about modern Giant Killers. *Poshlust*, it should be repeated, is especially vigorous and vicious when the sham is *not* obvious and when the values it mimics are considered, rightly or wrongly, to belong to the very highest level of art, thought or emotion. It is those books which are so *poshlustily* reviewed in the literary supplement of daily papers—the best sellers, the "stirring, profound and beautiful" novels; it is these "elevated and powerful" books that contain and distill the very essence of *poshlust*. I happen to have upon my desk a copy of a paper with a whole page advertising a certain novel, which novel is a fake from beginning to end and by its style, its ponderous gambols around elevated ideas, and absolute ignorance of what authentic literature was, is and always will be, strangely reminds one of the swan-fondling swimmer depicted by Gogol. "You lose yourself in it completely,"—says one reviewer;—"When the last page is turned you come back to the world of everyday a little thoughtful, as after a great experience" (note the coy "a little" and the perfectly automatic "as after a great"). "A singing book, compact of grace and light and

68

ecstasy, a book of pearly radiance,"—whispers another
(that swimmer was also "compact of grace," and the
swans had a "pearly radiance, too"). "The work of a master psychologist who can skillfully probe the very inner
recesses of men's souls." This "inner" (mind you—not
"outer"), and the other two or three delightful details
already mentioned are in exact conformity to the true
value of the book. In fact, this praise is perfectly adequate: the "beautiful" novel is "beautifully" reviewed and
the circle of *poshlust* is complete—or would be complete
had not words taken a subtle revenge of their own and
smuggled the truth in by secretly forming most nonsensi-
cal and most damning combinations while the reviewer
and publisher are quite sure that they are praising the
book, "which the reading public has made a (here follows
an enormous figure apparently meaning the quantity of
copies sold) triumph." For in the kingdom of *poshlust*
it is not the book that "makes a triumph" but the "reading public" which laps it up, blurb and all.

The particular novel referred to here may have been a
perfectly honest and sincere (as the saying goes) attempt
on the author's part to write something he felt strongly
about—and very possibly no commercial aspirations assisted him in that unfortunate process. The trouble is
that sincerity, honesty and even true kindness of heart
cannot prevent the demon of *poshlust* from possessing
himself of an author's typewriter when the man lacks
genius and when the "reading public" is what publishers
think it is. The dreadful thing about *poshlust* is that
one finds it so difficult to explain to people why a
particular book which seems chock-full of noble emotion

69

and compassion, and can hold the reader's attention "on a theme far removed from the discordant events of the day" is far, far worse than the kind of literature which *everybody* admits is cheap.

From the various examples collected here it will be I hope clear that *poshlust* is not only the obviously trashy but also the falsely important, the falsely beautiful, the falsely clever, the falsely attractive. A list of literary characters personifying *poshlust* (and thus namable in Russian *poshlyaki* in the case of males and *poshlyáchki* in the case of females—and rhyming with "key" and "latchkey" respectively) will include Polonius and the royal pair in Hamlet, Flaubert's Rodolphe and Homais, Laevsky in Chekhov's *Duel*, Joyce's Marion Bloom, young Bloch in *A la Recherche du Temps Perdu*, Maupassant's "Bel Ami," Anna Karenina's husband, Berg in *War and Peace* and numerous other figures in universal fiction. Socially minded Russian critics saw in *Dead Souls* and in *The Government Inspector* a condemnation of the social *poshlust* emanating from serf-owning bureaucratic provincial Russia and thus missed the true point. Gogol's heroes merely happen to be Russian squires and officials; their imagined surroundings and social conditions are perfectly unimportant factors—just as Monsieur Homais might be a business man in Chicago or Mrs. Bloom the wife of a schoolmaster in Vyshny-Volochok. Moreover, their surroundings and conditions, whatever they might have been in "real life," underwent such a thorough permutation and reconstruction in the laboratory of Gogol's peculiar genius that (as has been observed already in connection with *The Government Inspector*) it is as useless to

70

look in *Dead Souls* for an authentic Russian background
as it would be to try and form a conception of Denmark
on the basis of that little affair in cloudy Elsinore. And if
you want "facts," then let us inquire what experience had
Gogol of provincial Russia. Eight hours in a Podolsk inn,
a week in Kursk, the rest he had seen from the window of
his traveling carriage, and to this he had added the mem-
ories of his essentially Ukrainian youth spent in Mirgorod,
Nezhin, Poltava—all of which towns lay far outside Chichikov's itinerary. What seems true however is that *Dead
Souls* provides an attentive reader with a collection of
bloated dead souls belonging to *poshlyaki* and *poshlyáchki* described with that Gogolian gusto and wealth
of weird detail which lift the whole thing to the level of
a tremendous epic poem; and "poem" is in fact the subtle
subtitle appended by Gogol to *Dead Souls*. There is something sleek and plump about *poshlust*, and this gloss,
these smooth curves, attracted the artist in Gogol. The
immense spherical *poshlyak* (singular of the word) Paul
Chichikov eating the fig at the bottom of the milk which
he drinks to mellow his throat, or dancing in his night-
gown in the middle of the room while things on shelves
rock in response to his Lacedaemonian jig (ending in his
ecstatically hitting his chubby behind—his real face—
with the pink heel of his bare foot, thus propelling himself into the true paradise of dead souls) these are visions
which transcend the lesser varieties of *poshlust* discernible in humdrum provincial surroundings or in the petty
iniquities of petty officials. But a *poshlyak* even of Chichikov's colossal dimensions inevitably has somewhere in
him a hole, a chink through which you see the worm, the

71

little shriveled fool that lies all huddled up in the depth of the *poshlust*-painted vacuum. There was something faintly silly from the very start about that idea of buying up dead souls,—souls of serfs who had died since the last census and for whom their owners continued to pay the poll-tax, thus endowing them with a kind of abstract existence which however was quite concretely felt by the squire's pocket and could be just as "concretely" exploited by Chichikov, the buyer of such phantasma. This faint but rather sickening silliness was for a certain time concealed by the maze of complex machinations. *Morally* Chichikov was hardly guilty of any special crime in attempting to buy up dead men in a country where live men were lawfully purchased and pawned. If I paint my face with home made Prussian Blue instead of applying the Prussian Blue which is sold by the state and cannot be manufactured by private persons, my crime will be hardly worth a passing smile and no writer will make of it a Prussian Tragedy. But if I have surrounded the whole business with a good deal of mystery and flaunted a cleverness that presupposed most intricate difficulties in perpetrating a crime of that kind, and if owing to my letting a garrulous neighbor peep at my pots of home-brewn paint I get arrested and am roughly handled by men with authentic blue faces, then the laugh for what it is worth is on me. In spite of Chichikov's fundamental irreality in a fundamentally unreal world, the fool in him is apparent because from the very start he commits blunder upon blunder. It was silly to try to buy dead souls from an old woman who was afraid of ghosts; it was an incredible lapse of acumen to suggest such a

72

OUR MR. CHICHIKOV

Queer Street deal to the braggard and bully Nozdryov. I repeat however for the benefit of those who like books to provide them with "real people" and "real crime" and a "message" (that horror of horrors borrowed from the jargon of quack reformers) that *Dead Souls* will get them nowhere. Chichikov's guilt being a purely conventional matter, his destiny can hardly provoke any emotional reaction on our part. This is an additional reason why the view taken by Russian readers and critics, who saw in *Dead Souls* a matter-of-fact description of existing conditions, seems so utterly and ludicrously wrong. But when the legendary *poshlyak* Chichikov is considered as he ought to be, i. e. as a creature of Gogol's special brand moving in a special kind of Gogolian coil, the abstract notion of swindling in this serf-pawning business takes on strange flesh and begins to mean much more than it did when we considered it in the light of social conditions peculiar to Russia a hundred years ago. The dead souls he is buying are not merely names on a slip of paper. They are the dead souls that fill the air of Gogol's world with their leathery flutter, the clumsy animula of Manilov or of Korobochka, of the housewives of the town of N., of countless other little people bobbing throughout the book. Chichikov himself is merely the ill-paid representative of the Devil, a traveling salesman from Hades, "our Mr. Chichikov" as the Satan & Co. firm may be imagined calling their easy-going, healthy-looking but inwardly shivering and rotting agent. The *poshlust* which Chichikov personifies is one of the main attributes of the Devil, in whose existence, let it be added, Gogol believed far more seriously than he did in that of God. The chink in

Chichikov's armor, that rusty chink emitting a faint but dreadful smell (a punctured can of conserved lobster tampered with and forgotten by some meddling fool in the pantry) is the organic aperture in the devil's armor. It is the essential stupidity of universal *poshlust*.

Chichikov is doomed from the start and he rolls to that doom with a slight wobble in his gait which only the *poshlyaki* and *postlyáchkis* of the town of N. are capable of finding genteel and pleasant. At important moments when he launches upon one of those sententious speeches (with a slight break in his juicy voice—the tremolo of "dear brethren"), that are meant to drown his real intentions in a treacle of pathos, he applies to himself the words "despicable worm" and, curiously enough, a real worm is gnawing at his vitals and becomes suddenly visible if we squint a little when peering at his rotundity. I am reminded of a certain poster in old Europe that advertised automobile tires and featured something like a human being entirely made of concentric rings of rubber; and likewise, rotund Chichikov may be said to be formed of the tight folds of a huge flesh-colored worm.

If the special gruesome character attending the main theme of the book has been conveyed and if the different aspects of *poshlust* which I have noted at random have become connected in such a way as to form an artistic phenomenon (its Gogolian leitmotiv being the "roundness" of *poshlust*), then *Dead Souls* will cease to mimic a humorous tale or a social indictment and henceforth may be adequately discussed. So let us look at the pattern a little more closely.

74

3

"The gates of the hostelry in the governmental town of N. [so the book begins] admitted a smallish fairly elegant *britzka* on springs, of the sort used by bachelors such as retired colonels, staff-captains, country squires who own about a hundred souls of peasants—in short by all those who are dubbed 'gentlemen of medium quality.' Sitting in the *britzka* was a gentleman whose countenance could not be termed handsome, yet neither was he ill-favored: he was not too stout, nor was he too thin; you could not call him old, just as you could not say that he was still youthful. His arrival produced no stir whatever in the town and was not accompanied by anything unusual; alone two Russian *muzhiks* who were standing at the door of a dram-shop opposite the inn made certain remarks which however referred more to the carriage than to the person seated therein. 'Look at that wheel there,' said one. 'Now what do you think—would that wheel hold out as far as Moscow if need be, or would it not?' 'It would,' answered the other. 'And what about Kazan— I think it would not last that far?' 'It would not,'—answered the other. Upon this the conversation came to a close. And moreover, as the carriage drove up to the inn, a young man chanced to pass wearing white twill trousers that were very tight and short and a swallow-tail coat with claims to fashion from under which a shirtfront was visible fastened with a Tula bronze pin in the shape of a pistol. The young man turned his head, looked back at the carriage, caught hold of his cap, which the wind was about to blow off, and then went his way."

The conversation of the two "Russian *muzhiks*" (a typical Gogolian pleonasm) is purely speculative—a point which the abominable Fisher Unwin and Thomas Y. Crowell translations of course miss. It is a kind of to-be-or-not-to-be meditation in a primitive form. The speakers do not know whether the *britzka* is going to Moscow or not, just as Hamlet did not trouble to look whether, perhaps, he had not mislaid his bodkin. The *muzhiks* are not interested in the question of the precise itinerary that the britzka will follow; what fascinates them is solely the ideal problem of fixing the imaginary instability of a wheel in terms of imaginary distances; and this problem is raised to the level of sublime abstraction by their not knowing the exact distance from N. (an imaginary point) to Moscow, Kazan or Timbuctoo—and caring less. They impersonate the remarkable creative faculty of Russians, so beautifully disclosed by Gogol's own inspiration, of working in a void. Fancy is fertile only when it is futile. The speculation of the two *muzhiks* is based on nothing tangible and leads to no material results; but philosophy and poetry are born that way; meddlesome critics looking for a moral might conjecture that the rotundity of Chichikov is bound to come to grief, being symbolized by the rotundity of that doubtful wheel. Andrey Bely, who was a meddler of genius, saw in fact the whole first volume of *Dead Souls* as a closed circle whirling on its axle and blurring the spokes, with the theme of the wheel cropping up at each new revolution on round Chichikov's part. Another special touch is exemplified by the chance passer-by —that young man portrayed with a sudden and wholly irrelevant wealth of detail: he comes there as if he was

going to stay in the book (as so many of Gogol's homunculi seem intent to do—and do not). With any other
writer of his day the next paragraph would have been
bound to begin: "Ivan, for that was the young man's
name". . . But no: a gust of wind interrupts his stare
and he passes, never to be mentioned again. The faceless
saloon-walker in the next passage (whose movements are
so quick as he welcomes the newcomers that you cannot
discern his features) is again seen a minute later coming
down from Chichikov's room and spelling out the name
on a slip of paper as he walks down the steps. "Pa-vel
I-va-no-vich Chi-chi-kov"; and these syllables have a taxo-
nomic value for the identification of that particular stair-
case.

When speaking of *The Government Inspector* I found
pleasure in rounding up those peripheral characters that
enliven the texture of its background. Such characters in
Dead Souls as the inn-servant or Chichikov's valet (who
had a special smell of his own which he imparted at once
to his variable lodgings) do not quite belong to that class
of Little People. With Chichikov himself and the country
squires he meets they share the front stage of the book
although they speak little and have no visible influence
upon the course of Chichikov's adventures. Technically
speaking, the creation of peripheral personages in the play
was mainly dependent upon this or that character alluding
to people who never emerged from the wings. In a novel
the lack of action or speech on the part of secondary characters would not have been sufficient to endow them with
that kind of backstage existence, there being no footlights
to stress their actual absence from the front place. Gogol

77

however had another trick up his sleeve. The peripheral characters of his novel are engendered by the subordinate clauses of its various metaphors, comparisons and lyrical outbursts. We are faced by the remarkable phenomenon of mere forms of speech directly giving rise to live creatures. This is perhaps the most typical example of how this happens.

"Even the weather had obligingly accommodated itself to the setting: the day was neither bright nor gloomy but of a kind of bluey-grey tint such as is found only upon the worn-out uniforms of garrison soldiers, for the rest a peaceful class of warriors except for their being somewhat inebriate on Sundays."

It is not easy to render the curves of this life-generating syntax in plain English so as to bridge the logical, or rather biological, hiatus between a dim landscape under a dull sky and a groggy old soldier accosting the reader with a rich hiccup on the festive outskirts of the very same sentence. Gogol's trick consists in using as a link the word *"vprochem"* ("for the rest," "otherwise," *"d'ailleurs"*) which is a connection only in the grammatical sense but mimics a logical link, the word "soldiers" alone affording a faint pretext for the juxtaposition of "peaceful"; and as soon as this false bridge of *"vprochem"* has accomplished its magical work these mild warriors cross over, staggering and singing themselves into that peripheral existence with which we are already familiar.

When Chichikov comes to a party at the Governor's house, the chance mention of black-coated gentlemen crowding around the powdered ladies in a brilliant light leads to a fairly innocent looking comparison with buzzing flies—and the very next instant another life breaks through:

"The black tailcoats flickered and fluttered, separately and in clusters, this way and that, just as flies flutter over dazzling white chunks of sugar on a hot July day when the old housekeeper [here we are] hacks and divides it into sparkling lumps in front of the open window: all the children [second generation now!] look on as they gather about her, watching with curiosity the movements of her rough hands while the *airy* squadrons of flies that the light *air* [one of those repetitions so innate in Gogol's style that years of work over every passage could not eradicate them] has raised, fly boldly in, complete mistresses of the premises [or literally: 'full mistresses,' 'polnya khozyaiki,' which Isabel F. Hapgood in the Crowell edition mistranslates as 'fat housewives'] and, taking advantage of the old woman's purblindness and of the sun troubling her eyes, spread all over the dainty morsels, here separately, there in dense clusters."

It will be noticed that whereas the dull weather plus drunken trooper image comes to an end somewhere in the dusty suburban distance (where Ukhovyortov, the Ear-Twister, reigns) here, in the simile of the flies, which is a parody of the Homeric rambling comparison, a complete circle is described, and after his complicated and dangerous somersault, with no net spread under him, as other acrobatic authors have, Gogol manages to twist back to the initial "separately and in clusters." Several years ago during a Rugby game in England I saw the wonderful Obolensky kick the ball away on the run and then changing his mind, plunge forward and catch it back

with his hands . . . something of this kind of feat is performed by Nikolai Vassilievich. Needless to say that all
these things (in fact whole paragraphs and pages) were
left out by Mr. T. Fisher Unwin who to the "considerable
joy" of Mr. Stephen Graham (see preface, edition of 1915,
London) consented to re-publish *Dead Souls*. Incidentally, Graham thought that "*Dead Souls* is Russia herself"
and that Gogol "became a rich man and could winter at
Rome and Baden-Baden."

The lusty barking of dogs which met Chichikov as he
drove up to Madame Korobochka's house proves equally
fertile:

"Meanwhile the dogs were lustily barking in all possible
tones: one of them, with his head thrown back, indulged
in such conscientious ululations as if he were receiving
some prodigious pay for his labors; another hammered it
out cursorily like your village sexton; in between rang out,
similar to the bell of a mailcoach, the persistent treble of
what was probably a young whelp; and all this was
capped by a basso voice belonging presumably to some
old fellow endowed with a tough canine disposition, for
his voice was as hoarse as that of a basso profundo in a
church choir, when the concerto is in full swing with the
tenors straining on tiptoe in their eagerness to produce
a high note and all the rest, too, throwing their heads back
and striving upwards—while he alone with his bristly
chin thrust into his neckerchief, turns his knees out, sinks
down almost to the ground and issues thence that note
of his which makes the window-panes quake and rattle."

Thus the bark of a dog breeds a church chorister. In
yet another passage (where Paul arrives at Sobakevich's

house) a musician is born in a more complicated way re-mindful of the "dull sky drunken trooper" simile.

"As he drove up to the porch he noticed two faces which almost simultaneously appeared at the window: one belonged to a woman in a ribboned cap and it was as narrow and long as a cucumber; the other was a man's face, and round and broad it was, like those Moldavian pumpkins, called *gorlyanki* from which in our good country *balalaikas* are made, two-stringed light *balalaikas*, the adornment and delight of a nimble young rustic just out of his teens, the cock of his walk and a great one at whistling through his teeth and winking his eye at the white-bosomed and white-necked country-lasses who cluster around in order to listen to the delicate twanging of his strings." (This young yokel was transformed by Isabel Hapgood in her translation into "the susceptible youth of twenty who walks blinking along in his dandified way.")

The complicated maneuver executed by the sentence in order to have a village musician emerge from burly Sobakevich's head consists of three stages: the comparison of that head to a special kind of pumpkin, the transformation of that pumpkin into a special kind of *balalaika*, and finally the placing of that *balalaika* in the hands of a young villager who forthwith starts softly playing as he sits on a log with crossed legs (in brand new high boots) surrounded by sunset midgets and country girls. Especially remarkable is the fact that this lyrical digression is prompted by the appearance of what may seem to the casual reader to be the most matter-of-fact and stolid character of the book.

Sometimes the comparison-generated character is in

such a hurry to join in the life of the book that the metaphor ends in delightful bathos:

"A drowning man, it is said, will catch at the smallest chip of wood because at the moment he has not the presence of mind to reflect that hardly even a fly could hope to ride astride that chip, whereas he weighs almost a hundred and fifty pounds if not a good two hundred."

Who is that unfortunate bather, steadily and uncannily growing, adding weight, fattening himself on the marrow of a metaphor? We never shall know—but he almost managed to gain a footing.

The simplest method such peripheral characters employ to assert their existence is to take advantage of the author's way of stressing this or that circumstance or condition by illustrating it with some striking detail. The picture starts living a life of its own—rather like that leering organ-grinder with whom the artist in H. G. Wells' story *The Portrait* struggled, by means of jabs and splashes of green paint when the portrait he was making became alive and disorderly. Observe for instance the ending of Chapter 7, where the intention is to convey the impressions of night falling upon a peaceful provincial town. Chichikov after successfully clinching his ghostly deal with the landowners has been entertained by the worthies of the town and goes to bed very drunk; his coachman and his valet quietly depart on a private spree of their own, then stumble back to the inn, most courteously propping up each other, and soon go to sleep too.

". . . emitting snores of incredible density of sound, echoed from the neighboring room by their master's thin nasal wheeze. Soon after this everything quieted down and deep slumber enveloped the hostelry; one light alone remained burning and that was in the small window of a certain lieutenant who had arrived from Ryazan and who was apparently a keen amateur of boots inasmuch as he had already acquired four pairs and was persistently trying on a fifth one. Every now and again he would go up to his bed as though he intended to take them off and lie down; but he simply could not; in truth those boots were well made; and for a long while still he kept on revolving his foot and inspecting the dashing cut of an admirably finished heel."

Thus the chapter ends—and that lieutenant is still trying on his immortal jackboot, and the leather glistens, and the candle burns straight and bright in the only lighted window of a dead town in the depth of a star-dusted night. I know of no more lyrical description of nocturnal quiet than this Rhapsody of the Boots.

The same kind of spontaneous generation occurs in Chapter 9, when the author wishes to convey with special strength the bracing turmoil which the rumors surrounding the acquisition of dead souls provoked throughout the province. Country squires who for years had been lying curled up in their holes like so many dormice all of a sudden blinked and crawled out:

"There appeared a certain Sysoy Paphnutyevich, and a certain Macdonald Carlovich [a singular name to say the least but necessary here to underline utter remoteness from life and the consequent irreality of that person, a dream in a dream, so to speak], about whom nobody had heard before; and a long lean impossibly tall fellow [literally: 'a certain long long one, of such tall stature as had

83

never been even seen'] with a bullet wound in his hand . . ."

In the same chapter, after explaining at length that he will name no names because "whatever name be invented there is quite sure to crop up in some corner of our empire —which is big enough for all purposes—some person who bears it, and who is sure to be mortally offended and to declare that the author sneaked in with the express intention of nosing out every detail," Gogol cannot stop the two voluble ladies whom he sets chattering about the Chichikov mystery from divulging their names as if his characters actually escaped his control and blurted out what he wished to conceal. Incidentally, one of those passages which fairly burst with little people tumbling out and scattering all over the page (or straddling Gogol's pen like a witch riding a broomstick) reminds one in a curious anachronistic fashion of a certain intonation and trick of style used by Joyce in *Ulysses* (but then Sterne too used the abrupt question and circumstantial answer method).

"Our hero however was utterly unconscious of this [i.e. that he was boring with his sententious patter a certain young lady in a ballroom] as he went on telling her all kinds of pleasant things which he had happened to utter on similar occasions in various places. [Where?] In the Government of Simbirsk, at the house of Sophron Ivanovich Bezpechnoy, where the latter's daughter, Adelaida Sophronovna, was also present with her three sisters-in-law, Maria Gavrilovna, Alexandra Gavrilovna and Adelheida Gavrilovna; at the house of Frol Vassilyevich Pobedonosnoy, in the Government of Pensa; and at that of the latter's brother, where the following were present: his wife's sister Katherina Mikhailovna and her cousins, Rosa Feodorovna and Emilia Feodorovna; in the Government of Viatka, at the house of Piotr Varsonophyevich, where his daughter-in-law's sister Pelagea Egorovna was present, together with a niece, Sophia Rostislavna and two step-sisters: Sophia Alexandrovna and Maclatura Alexandrovna."

Through some of these names runs that curious foreign strain (quasi-German in this case) which Gogol generally employs to convey a sense of remoteness and optical distortion due to the haze; queer hybrid names fit for difform or not yet quite formed people; and while squire Bespechnoy and squire Pobedonosnoy are, so to speak, only slightly *drunken* names (meaning as they do "Unconcerned" and "Victorious") the last one on the list is an apotheosis of nightmare nonsense faintly echoed by the Russian Scotsman whom we have already admired. It is inconceivable what type of mind one must have to see in Gogol a forerunner of the "naturalistic school" and a "realistic painter of life in Russia."

Not only people, but things too indulge in these nomenclatorial orgies. Notice the pet names that the officials of the town of N. give to their playing cards. *Chervy* means "hearts"; but it also sounds very much like "worms," and with the linguistic inclination of Russians to pull out a word to its utmost length for the sake of emotional emphasis, it becomes *chervotochina*, which means worm-eaten core. *Piki*—"spades"—French *piques*—turn into *pikentia*, that is, assume a jocular dog-Latin ending; or they produce such variations as *pikendras* (false Greek

85

ending) or *pichura* (a faint ornithological shade), sometimes magnified into *pichurishchuk* (the bird turning as
it were into an antediluvian lizard, thus reversing the order of natural evolution). The utter vulgarity and autom-
atism of these grotesque nicknames, most of which Gogol invented himself, attracted him as a remarkable means
to disclose the mentality of those who used them.

4

The difference between human vision and the image
perceived by the faceted eye of an insect may be compared with the difference between a half-tone block made
with the very finest screen and the corresponding picture
as represented by the very coarse screening used in
common newspaper pictorial reproduction. The same
comparison holds good between the way Gogol saw
things and the way average readers and average writers
see things. Before his and Pushkin's advent Russian literature was purblind. What form it perceived was an outline
directed by reason: it did not see color for itself but
merely used the hackneyed combinations of blind noun
and dog-like adjective that Europe had inherited from
the ancients. The sky was blue, the dawn red, the foliage
green, the eyes of beauty black, the clouds grey, and so
on. It was Gogol (and after him Lermontov and Tolstoy)
who first saw yellow and violet at all. That the sky could
be pale green at sunrise, or the snow a rich blue on a
cloudless day, would have sounded like heretical nonsense
to your so-called "classical" writer, accustomed as he was
to the rigid conventional color-schemes of the Eighteenth

Century French school of literature. Thus the development of the art of description throughout the centuries may be profitably treated in terms of vision, the faceted eye becoming a unified and prodigiously complex organ and the dead dim "accepted colors" (in the sense of "idées reçues") yielding gradually their subtle shades and allowing new wonders of application. I doubt whether any writer, and certainly not in Russia, had ever noticed before, to give the most striking instance, the moving pattern of light and shade on the ground under trees or the tricks of color played by sunlight with leaves. The following description of Plushkin's garden in *Dead Souls* shocked Russian readers in much the same way as Manet did the bewhiskered philistines of his day.

"An extensive old garden which stretched behind the house and beyond the estate to lose itself in the fields, alone seemed, rank and rugged as it was, to lend a certain freshness to these extensive grounds and alone was completely picturesque in its vivid wildness. The united tops of trees that had grown wide in liberty spread above the skyline in masses of green clouds and irregular domes of tremulous leafage. The colossal white trunk of a birchtree deprived of its top, which had been broken off by some gale or thunderbolt, rose out of these dense green masses and disclosed its rotund smoothness in midair, like a well proportioned column of sparkling marble; the oblique, sharply pointed fracture in which, instead of a capital, it terminated above, showed black against its snowy whiteness like some kind of headpiece or a dark bird. Strands of hop, after strangling the bushes of elder, mountain ash and hazel below, had meandered all over the ridge of the

87

fence whence they ran up at last to twist around that trun-
cate birchtree halfway up its length. Having reached its
middle, they hung down from there and were already beginning to catch at the tops of other trees, or had sus-
pended in the air their intertwined loops and thin cling-
ing hooks which were gently oscillated by the air. Here
and there the green thicket broke asunder in a blaze of
sunshine and showed a deep unlighted recess in between,
similar to dark gaping jaws; this vista was all shrouded in
shadow and all one could discern in its black depth was:
the course of a narrow footpath, a crumbling balustrade,
a toppling summer-house, the hollow trunk of a decrepit
willow, a thick growth of hoary sedge bristling out from
behind it, an intercrossment and tangle of twigs and
leaves that had lost their sap in this impenetrable wild-
wood, and lastly, a young branch of maple which had
projected sideways the green paws of its leaves, under one
of which a gleam of sunlight had somehow managed to
creep in after all, unexpectedly making of that leaf a
translucid and resplendent marvel burning in the dense
darkness.

"On the very edge of the garden several great aspens
stood apart, lording it over the rest, with the huge nests of
crows propped up by their tremulous summits. On some
of these trees dislocated boughs that were not quite de-
tached from the trunks hung down together with their
shriveled foliage. In a word all was beautiful as neither
nature nor art can contrive, beautiful as it only is when
these two come together, with nature giving the final
touch of her chisel to the work of man (that more often
than not he has piled up anyhow), alleviating its bulky

agglomeration and suppressing both its crudely obvious regularity and the miserable gaps through which its stark background clearly showed and casting a wonderful warmth over all that had been evolved in the bleakness of measured neatness and propriety."

I do not wish to contend that my translation is especially good or that its clumsiness corresponds to Gogol's disheveled grammar, but at least it is exact in regard to sense. It is entertaining to glance at the mess which my predecessors have made of this wonderful passage. Isabel Hapgood (1885) for instance, who at least attempted to translate it in toto, heaps blunder upon blunder, turning the Russian "birch" into the non-endemic "beech," the "aspen" into an "ashtree," the "elder" into "lilac," the "dark bird" into a "blackbird," the "gaping" (ziyavshaya) into "shining" (which would have been siyavshaya), etc. etc.

5

The various attributes of the characters help to expand them in a kind of spherical way to the remotest regions of the book. Chichikov's aura is continued and symbolized by his snuffbox and his traveling case; by that "silver and enamel snuffbox" which he offered generously to everybody and on the bottom of which people could notice a couple of violets delicately placed there for the sake of their additional perfume (just as he would rub on Sunday mornings his sub-human, obscene body, as white and as plump as that of some fat woodboring larva, with eau de cologne—the last sickly sweet whiff of the smuggling business of his hidden past); for Chichikov is a fake and

89

a phantom clothed in a pseudo-Pickwickian rotundity of
flesh, and trying to smother the miserable reek of inferno
(something far worse than the "natural smell" of his
moody valet) permeating him, by means of maudlin perfumes pleasing to the grotesque noses of the inhabitants
of that nightmare town. And the traveling chest:

"The author feels sure that among his readers there are
some curious enough to be desirous of knowing the plan
and inner arrangement of that chest. Being anxious to
please he sees no reason to deny them their satisfaction.
Here it is, this inner arrangement."

And without having warned the reader that what follows is not a box at all but a circle in hell and the exact
counterpart of Chichikov's horribly rotund soul (and that
what he, the author, is about to undertake is the disclosure
of Chichikov's innards under a bright lamp in a vivisec-
tor's laboratory), he continues thus:

"In the center was a soap-container [Chichikov being
a soap bubble blown by the devil]; beyond the soap-
container were six or seven narrow little interspaces for
razors [Chichikov's chubby cheeks were always silky-
smooth: a fake cherub], then two square niches for sand-
box and inkstand, with little troughs for pens, sealing wax
and all things that were longish in shape [the scribe's in-
struments for collecting dead souls]; then all sorts of compartments with and without lids, for shortish things; these
were full of visiting cards, funeral notices, theatre tickets
and such like slips which were stored up as souvenirs
[Chichikov's social flutters]. All this upper tray with its
various compartments could be taken out, and beneath
it was a space occupied by piles of paper in sheets [paper

being the devil's main medium of intercourse]; then followed a small secret drawer for money. This could be slipped out inconspicuously from the side of the chest [Chichikov's heart]. It would always be drawn out and pushed back so quickly by its owner [systole and diastole] that it is impossible to say exactly how much money it contained [even the author does not know]."

Andrey Bely, following up one of those strange subconscious clues which are discoverable only in the works of authentic genius, noted that this box was the *wife* of Chichikov (who otherwise was as impotent as all Gogol's subhuman heroes) in the same way as the cloak was Akaky's mistress in *The Overcoat* or the belfry Shponka's mother-in-law in *Ivan Shponka and his Aunt*. It may be further observed that the name of the only female landowner in the book, "Squiress" Korobochka means "little box"—in fact, Chichikov's "little box" (reminding one of Harpagon's ejaculation: "Ma cassette!" in Molière's *L'Avare*); and Korobochka's arrival in the town at the crucial moment is described in buxological terms, subtly in keeping with those used for the above quoted anatomic preparation of Chichikov's soul. Incidentally the reader ought to be warned that for the true appreciation of these passages he must quite forget any kind of Freudian nonsense that may have been falsely suggested to him by these chance references to connubial relations. Andrey Bely has a grand time making fun of solemn psychoanalysts.

We shall first note that in the beginning of the following remarkable passage (perhaps the greatest one in the whole book) a reference to the night breeds a peripheral character in the same way as it did the Amateur of Boots.

"But in the meantime, while he [Chichikov] sat in his uncomfortable armchair, a prey to troublesome thoughts and insomnia, vigorously cursing Nosdryov [who had been the first to disturb the inhabitants' peace of mind by bragging about Chichikov's strange commerce] and all Nosdryov's relatives [the 'family tree' which grows out spontaneously from our national kind of oath], in the faint glow of a tallow candle which threatened to go out any moment under the black cap that had formed long ago all over its wick, and while the dark night blindly stared into his windows ready to shade into blue as dawn approached, and distant cocks whistled to one another in the distance [note the repetition of 'distant' and the monstrous 'whistled': Chichikov, emitting a thin nasal whistling snore, is dozing off, and the world becomes blurred and strange, the snore mingling with the doubly-distant crowing of cocks, while the sentence itself writhes as it gives birth to a quasi-human being], and somewhere in the sleeping town there stumbled on perchance a freize overcoat—some poor devil wearing that overcoat [here we are], of unknown standing or rank, and who knew only one thing [in the text the verb stands in the feminine gender in accordance with the feminine gender of 'freize overcoat' which, as it were, has usurped the place of man]—that trail [to the pub] which, alas, the devil-may-care Russian nation has burnt so thoroughly,—in the meantime [the "meantime" of the beginning of this sentence] at the other end of town. . . ."

Let us pause here for a moment to admire the lone passer-by with his blue unshaven chin and red nose, so different in his sorry condition (corresponding to Chichikov's troubled mind) from the passionate dreamer who had delighted in a boot when Chichikov's sleep was so lusty. Gogol continues as follows:

". . . at the other end of the town there was happening something that was to make our hero's plight even worse. To wit: through remote streets and by-alleys of the town rumbled a most queer vehicle which it is doubtful anybody could have named more exactly. It looked neither like a *tarantas* [simplest kind of traveling carriage], nor like a calash, nor like a *britzka*, being in sooth more like a fat-cheeked very round watermelon set upon wheels [now comes a certain subtle correspondence to the description of round Chichikov's box]. The cheeks of this melon, that is, the carriage doors, that bore remnants of their former yellow varnish, closed very poorly owing to the bad state of the handles and locks which had been perfunctorily fixed up by means of string. The melon was filled with chintz cushions, small ones, long ones, and ordinary ones, and stuffed with bags containing loaves of bread and such eatables as *kalachi* [purse-shaped rolls], *kokoorki* [buns with egg or cheese stuffing], *skorodoomki* [skoro-dumplings] and *krendels* [a sort of magnified *kalach* in the form of a capital B, richly flavored and decorated]. A chicken-pie, and a *rassolnik* [a sophisticated giblet-pie] were visible even on the top of the carriage. The rear board was occupied by an individual that might have been originally a footman, dressed in a short coat of speckled homespun stuff, with a slightly hoary stubble on his chin, the kind of individual known by the appellation of 'boy' (though he might be over

93

fifty). The rattle and screech of the iron clamps and rusty screws awakened a police sentry at the other end of the town [another character is born here in the best Gogolian manner], who, raising his halberd, shocked himself out of his slumber with a mighty roar of 'Who goes there?', but upon becoming aware that nobody was passing and that only a faint rumble was coming from afar [the dream melon had passed into the dream town], he captured a beast of sorts right upon his collar and walking up to a lantern slew it on his thumbnail [i.e. by squashing it with the nail of the curved index of the same hand, the adopted system of Russians for dealing with hefty national fleas], after which he put his halberd aside and went to sleep again according to the rules of his particular knighthood [here Gogol catches up with the coach which he had let go by while busy with the sentry]. The horses every now and then fell on their foreknees not only because they were not shod but also because they were little used to comfortable town pavements. The rickety coach after turning this way and that down several streets, turned at last into a dark lane leading past the little parish church called Nikola-na-Nedotychkakh and stopped at the gate of the *protopopsha's* [priest's wife or widow] house. A kerchiefed and warmly clothed servant girl climbed out of the *britzka* [typical of Gogol: now that the nondescript vehicle has arrived at its destination, in a comparatively tangible world, it has become one of the definite species of carriages which he had been careful to say it was not] and using both her fists banged upon the gate with a vigor a man might have envied; the 'boy' in the speck-

94

led coat was dragged down somewhat later for he was sleeping the sleep of the dead. There was a barking of dogs, and at last the gates, gaping wide, swallowed, although not without difficulty, that clumsy traveling contrivance. The coach rolled into a narrow yard which was crammed with logs of wood, chicken coops and all sorts of cages; out of the carriage a lady emerged; this lady was a collegiate secretary's widow and a landowner herself: Madame Korobochka."

Madame Korobochka is as much like Cinderella as Paul Chichikov is like Pickwick. The melon she emerges from can hardly be said to be related to the fairy pumpkin. It becomes a *britzka* just before her emergence, probably for the same reason that the crowing of the cock became a whistling snore. One may assume that her arrival is seen through Chichikov's dream (as he dozes off in his uncomfortable armchair). She does come, in reality, but the appearance of her coach is slightly distorted by his dream (all his dreams being governed by the memory of the secret drawers of his box) and if this vehicle turns out to be a *britzka* it is merely because Chichikov had arrived in one too. Apart from these transformations the coach is round, because plump Chichikov is himself a sphere and all his dreams revolve round a constant center; and at the same time her coach is also his roundish traveling case. The plan and inner arrangement of the coach is revealed with the same devilish graduation as those of the box had been. The elongated cushions are the "long things" of the box; the fancy pastries correspond to the frivolous mementoes Paul preserved; the papers for

95

jotting down the dead souls acquired are weirdly symbolized by the drowsy serf in the speckled jacket; and the
secret compartment, Chichikov's heart, yields Korobochka
herself.

6

I have already alluded, in discussing comparison-born
characters, to the lyrical gust which follows immediately
upon the appearance of stolid Sobakevich's huge face,
from which face, as from some great ugly cocoon, emerges
a bright delicate moth. The fact is that, curiously enough,
Sobakevich, in spite of his solemnity and bulk, is the most
poetical character in the book, and this may require a certain amount of explanation. First of all here are the emblems and attributes of his being (he is visualized in terms
of furniture).

"As he took a seat, Chichikov glanced around at the
walls and at the pictures that hung upon them. All the
figures in these pictures were those of brawny fellows—
full length lithographic portraits of Greek generals: Mav-
rocordato resplendent in his red-trousered uniform, with
spectacles on his nose, Miaoulis, Kanaris. All these heroes
had such stout thighs and such prodigious mustachios
that it fairly gave one the creeps. In the midst of these
robust Greeks a place had been given, for no earthly reason or purpose, to the portrait of a thin wispy little Bagration [famous Russian general] who stood there above his
little banners and cannons in a miserably narrow frame.
Thereupon a Greek personage followed again, namely
the heroine Bobelina, whose mere leg seemed bigger than
the whole body of any of the fops that swarm in our mod-

ern drawing rooms. The owner being himself a hardy and hefty man apparently wished his room to be adorned with hardy and hefty people too."

But was this the only reason? Is there not something singular in this leaning towards romantic Greece on Sobakevich's part? Was there not a "thin wispy little" poet concealed in that burly breast? For nothing in those days provoked a greater emotion in poetically inclined Russians than Byron's quest.

"Chichikov glanced again around the room: everything in it was both solid and unwieldy to the utmost degree and bore a kind of resemblance to the owner of the house himself. In one corner a writing desk of walnut wood bulged out on its four most ridiculous legs—a regular bear. Table, chair, armchair—everything was of the most heavy and uncomfortable sort; in a word, every article, every chair seemed to be saying: 'and I also am Sobakevich!' or 'and I also am very much like Sobakevich!' "

The food he eats is fare fit for some uncouth giant. If there is pork he must have the whole pig served at table, if it is mutton then the whole sheep must be brought in; if it is goose, then the whole bird must be there. His dealings with food are marked by a kind of primeval poetry and if there can be said to exist a gastronomical rhythm, his prandial meter is the Homeric one. The half of the saddle of mutton that he dispatches in a few crunching and susurrous instants, the dishes that he engulfs next—pastries whose size exceeds that of one's plate and a turkey as big as a calf, stuffed with eggs, rice, liver and other rich ingredients—all these are the emblems, the outer crust and natural ornaments of the man and proclaim his

97

existence with that kind of hoarse eloquence that Flaubert used to put into his pet epithet "Hénorme." Sobakevich works in the food line with great slabs and mighty hacks, and the fancy jams served by his wife after supper are ignored by him as Rodin would not condescend to notice the rococo baubles in a fashionable boudoir.

"No soul whatever seemed to be present in that body, or if he did have a soul it was not where it ought to be, but, as in the case of Kashchey the Deathless [a ghoulish character in Russian folklore] it dwelled somewhere beyond the mountains and was hidden under such a thick crust, that anything that might have stirred in its depths could produce no tremor whatever on the surface."

7

The "dead souls" are revived twice: first through the medium of Sobakevich (who endows them with his own bulky attributes), then by Chichikov (with the author's lyrical assistance). Here is the first method—Sobakevich is boosting his wares:

" 'You just consider: what about the carriage-maker Mikheyev, for instance? Consider, every single carriage he used to make was complete with springs! And mind you, not the Moscow kind of work that gets undone in an hour, but solid, I tell you, and then he would upholster it, and varnish it too!' Chichikov opened his mouth to observe that however good Mikheyev might have been he had long ceased to exist; but Sobakevich was warming up to his subject, as they say; hence this rush and command of words.

" 'Or take Stepan Probka, the carpenter. I can wager my head that you will not find his like anywhere. Goodness, what strength that man had! Had he served in the Guards he would have got every blessed thing he wanted: the fellow was over seven feet high!

"Again Chichikov was about to remark that Probka too was no more; but Sobakevich seemed to have burst his dam: such torrents of speech followed that all one could do was to listen.

" 'Or Milyushkin, the bricklayer, he that could build a stove in almost any house! Or Maxim Telyatnikov, the shoemaker: with his awl he would prick a thing just once and there was a pair of boots for you; and what boots—they made you feel mighty grateful; and with all that, never swallowing a drop of liquor. Or Yeremey Sorokoplekhin—ah, that man could have stood his own against all the others: went to trade in Moscow and the tax alone he paid me was five hundred roubles every time.' "

Chichikov tries to remonstrate with this strange booster of non-existent wares, and the latter cools down somewhat, agreeing that the "souls" are dead, but then flares up again.

" 'Sure enough they are dead. . . . But on the other hand, what good are the live peasants of today? What sort of men are *they*? Mere flies—not men!'

" 'Yes, but anyway they can be said to exist, while those others are only figments.'

" 'Figments indeed! If only you had seen Mikheyev. . . . Ah, well, you are not likely to set eyes on anybody of that sort again. A great hulky mass that could hardly have squeezed into this room. In those great big shoulders of his there was more strength than in a horse. I should very much like to know where you could find another such figment!' "

Speaking thus Sobakevich turns to the portrait of Bagration as if asking the latter's advice; and some time later when, after a good deal of haggling the two are about to come to terms and there is a solemn pause, "eagle-nosed Bagration from his vantage point on the wall watched very attentively the clinching of the deal." This is the nearest we get to Sobakevich's soul while he is about, but a wonderful echo of the lyrical strain in his boorish nature may be discerned further on when Chichikov peruses the list of dead souls that the burly squire had sold him.

"And presently, when he glanced at these lists of names belonging to peasants who had really been peasants once, had labored and caroused, had been ploughmen and carriers, had cheated their owners, or perhaps had simply been good *muzhiks*, he was seized with a queer feeling which he could not explain to himself. Every list seemed to have a special character of its own, and consequently the peasants themselves seemed to acquire a special character. Almost all those that had belonged to Korobochka possessed various appendages and nicknames. Brevity distinguished Plushkin's list, where many of the peasants were merely defined by the initial syllables of their Christian names and patronymics followed by a couple of dots. Sobakevich's list struck one by its extraordinary completeness and wealth of detail. . . . 'Dear me,' said Chichikov to himself with a sudden gush of emotion peculiar to sentimental scoundrels, 'how many of you have been crowded in here! What sort of lives did you lead, my friends?' [He imagines these lives, and one by one the dead *muzhiks* leap into existence shoving chubby Chichikov aside and asserting themselves.] 'Ah, here he is, Stepan Probka, the giant who would have graced the Guards. I guess you have tramped across many provinces with your axe hanging from your belt and your boots slung over your shoulder [a Russian peasant's way of economizing on footgear], living upon a pennyworth of bread and some dry fish for the double of that, and bringing in every time, I guess, [to your master] at the bottom of your money bag, a hundred silver roubles or so, or perhaps a couple of banknotes sewed up in your canvas trousers or thrust deep into your boot. What manner of death was yours? Had you climbed right up to the domed roof of a church in trying to make more money [in wages for repairs] or had you perhaps hoisted yourself up to the very cross on that church, and did you slip from a beam thereon to dash your brains out on the ground whereat [some elderly comrade of yours] standing nearby only scratched the back of his head and said with a sigh: 'Well, my lad, you sure did have a fall'— and then tied a rope round his waist and climbed up to take your place. . . .'

" '. . . And what about you, Grigory Doyezhaï-ne-doye-desh [Drive-to-where-you-won't-get]? Did you ply a carrier's trade and having acquired a *troïka* [three horses] and a bast-covered *kibitka*, did you forsake forever your home, your native den, in order to trundle merchants to the fair? Did you surrender your soul to God on the road? Were you dispatched by your own comrades in a quarrel for the favors of some plump and ruddy beauty whose soldier husband was away? Or did those leathern gauntlets you wore and your three short-legged but sturdy steeds tempt a robber on some forest road? Or perhaps, after a good bit of desultory thinking as you lay in your bunk, you suddenly made for the pothouse, just like that, and then plunged straight into a hole in the ice of the river, never to be seen again?'"

The very name of one "Neoovazhaï-Koryto" (a weird combination of "disrespect" and "pigtrough") suggests by its uncouth straggling length the kind of death that had befallen this man: "A clumsy van drove over you as you were lying asleep in the middle of the road." The mention of a certain Popov, domestic serf in Plushkin's list, engenders a whole dialogue after it has been assumed that the man had probably received some education and so had been guilty (note this superlogical move) not of vulgar murder, but of genteel theft.

"'Very soon however some Rural Police Officer comes and arrests you for having no passport. You remain unconcerned during the confrontation. 'Who is your owner?' asks the Rural Police Officer, seasoning his question with a bit of strong language as befits the occasion. 'Squire So-and-so,' you reply briskly. 'Then what are you doing here [miles away],' asks the Rural Police Officer. 'I have been released on *obrok* [meaning that he had been permitted to work on his own or for some other party under the condition that he paid a percentage of his earnings to the squire who owned him], you reply without a moment's hesitation. 'Where is your passport?' 'My present boss, the merchant Pimenov, has it.' 'Let Pimenov be called! . . . You are Pimenov?' 'I am Pimenov.' 'Did he give you his passport?' 'No, he did nothing of the sort.' 'Why have you

102

been lying?' asks the Rural Police Officer with the addition of a bit of strong language. 'That's right,' you answer briskly, 'I did not give it him because I came home late— so I left it with Antip Prokhorov, the bellringer.' 'Let the bellringer be called!' 'Did he give you his passport?' 'No, I did not receive any passport from him.' 'Lying again,' says the Rural Police Officer, spicing his speech with a bit of strong language. 'Come now, where is that passport of yours?' 'I had it,' you answer promptly, 'but with one thing and another it is very likely I dropped it on the way.' 'And what about that army coat?' says the Rural Police Officer, again treating you to a bit of strong language. 'Why did you steal it? And why did you steal a trunk full of coppers from the priest?' "

It goes on like that for some time and then Popov is followed to the various prisons of which our great land has always been so prolific. But although these "dead souls" are brought back to life only to be led to misfortune and death, their resurrection is of course far more satisfactory and complete than the false "moral resurrection" which Gogol intended to stage in the projected second or third volumes for the benefit of pious and law-abiding citizens. His art through a whim of his own revived the dead in these passages. Ethical and religious considerations could only destroy the soft, warm, fat creatures of his fancy.

8

The emblems of rosy-lipped, blond, sentimental, vapid and slatternly Manilov (there is a suggestion of "mannerism" in his name and of *tuman* which means mist, besides the word *manil*, a verb expressing the idea of dreamy attraction) are: that greasy green scum on the pond among the maudlin charms of an "English garden" with its trimmed shrubs and blue pillared pavilion ("Temple of Solitary Meditation"); the pseudo-classical names which he gives to his children; that book permanently lying in his study, and opened permanently at the fourteenth page (not fifteenth, which might have implied some kind of decimal method in reading and not thirteenth which would have been the devil's dozen of pages, but *fourteenth*, an insipid pinkish-blond numeral with as little personality as Manilov himself); those careless gaps in the furniture of his house, where the armchairs had been upholstered with silk of which, however, there had not been enough for all, so that two of them were simply covered with coarse matting; those two candlesticks, one of which was very elegantly wrought of dark bronze with a trio of Grecian Graces and a mother-of-pearl shade, while the other was simply "a brass invalid," lame, crooked and besmeared with tallow; but perhaps the most appropriate emblem is the neat row of hillocks formed by the ashes that Manilov used to shake out of his pipe and arrange in symmetrical piles on the window-sill—the only artistic pleasure he knew.

9

"Happy is the writer who omits these dull and repulsive characters that disturb one by being so painfully real; who comes close to such that disclose the lofty virtue of man; who from the great turmoil of images that whirl daily around him selects but a few exceptions; who has been always faithful to the sublime harmony of his lyre, has never come down from those heights to visit his poor insignificant kinsmen and remained aloof, out of touch with the earth, wholly immersed in remote magnificent fancies. Ay, doubly enviable is his admirable lot: those visions are a home and a family to him; and at the same time the thunder of his fame rolls far and wide. The delicious mist of the incense he burns dims human eyes; the miracle of his flattery masks all the sorrows of life and depicts only the goodness of man. Applauding crowds come streaming in his wake to rush behind his triumphal chariot. He is called a great universal poet, soaring high above all other geniuses of the world even as an eagle soars above other high flying creatures. The mere sound of his name sends a thrill through ardent young hearts; all eyes greet him with the radiance of responsive tears. He has no equal in might; he is God.

"But a different lot and another fate await the writer who has dared to evoke all such things that are constantly before one's eyes but which idle eyes do not see—the shocking morass of trifles that has tied up our lives, and the essence of cold, crumbling, humdrum characters with whom our earthly way, now bitter, now dull, fairly swarms; has dared to make them prominently and brightly visible to the eyes of all men by means of the vigorous strength of his pitiless chisel. Not for him will be the applause, no grateful tears will he see, no souls will he excite with unanimous admiration; not to him will a girl of sixteen come flying, her head all awhirl with heroic fervor. Not for him will be that sweet enchantment when a poet hears nothing but the harmonies he has engendered himself; and finally, he will not escape the judgment of his time, the judgment of hypocritical and unfeeling contemporaries who will accuse the creatures his mind has bred of being base and worthless, will allot a contemptible nook to him in the gallery of those authors who insult mankind, will ascribe to him the morals of his own characters and will deny him everything, heart, soul and the divine flame of talent. For the judgment of his time does not admit that the lenses through which suns may be surveyed are as marvellous as those that disclose the movement of otherwise imperceptible insects; for the judgment of his time does not admit that a man requires a good deal of spiritual depth in order to be able to throw light upon an image supplied by base life and to turn it into an exquisite masterpiece; nor does the judgment of his time admit that lofty ecstatic laughter is quite worthy of taking its place beside the loftiest lyrical gust and that it has nothing in common with the faces a mountebank makes. The judgment of his time does not admit this and will twist everything into reproof and abuse directed against the unrecognized writer; deprived of assistance, response and sympathy, he will remain, like some homeless traveler alone on the road. Grim will be his career and bitterly will he realize his utter loneliness. . . .

"And for a long time yet, led by some wondrous power, I am fated to journey hand in hand with my strange heroes and to survey the surging immensity of life, to survey it through the laughter that all can see and through unknown invisible tears. And still far away is that time when with a gushing force of a different origin the formidable blizzard of inspiration will rise from my austere and blazing brow and, in a sacred tremor, humans will harken to the sublime thunder of a different speech."

Immediately after this extravagant eloquence, which is like a blaze of light revealing a glimpse of what at the time Gogol expected to be able to do in the second volume of his work, there follows the diabolically grotesque scene of fat Chichikov, half naked, dancing a jig in his bedroom —which is not quite the right kind of example to prove that "ecstatic laughter" and "lyrical gusts" are good companions in Gogol's book. In fact Gogol deceived himself if he thought that he could laugh that way. Nor are the lyrical outbursts really parts of the solid pattern of the book; they are rather those natural interspaces without which the pattern would not be what it is. Gogol indulges in the pleasure of being blown off his feet by the gale that comes from some other clime of his world, (the Alpine-italianate part), just as in *The Government Inspector* the modulated cry of the invisible reinsman ("Heigh, my winged ones!") brought in a whiff of summer night air, a sense of remoteness and romance, an *invitation au voyage*.

The main lyrical note of *Dead Souls* bursts into existence when the idea of Russia as Gogol saw Russia (a peculiar landscape, a special atmosphere, a symbol, a long, long road) looms in all its strange loveliness through the tremendous dream of the book. It is important to note that the following passage is sandwiched between Chichikov's final departure, or rather escape, from the town (which had been set upside down by the rumors of his deal) and the description of his early years.

"Meanwhile the *britzka* had turned into emptier streets;

107

soon, only fences [a Russian fence is a blind grey affair more or less evenly serrated on top and resembling
in this the distant line of a Russian firwood] stretched
their wooden lengths and foretold the end of the town
[in space, not in time]. See, the pavement comes to an
end and here is the town barrier ["Schlagbaum": a mov-
able pole painted with white and black stripes] and the
town is left behind, and there is nothing around, and we
are again travelers on the road. And again on both sides of
the highway there comes an endless succession of mileposts, post station officials, wells, burdened carts, drab
hamlets with samovars, peasant women and some bearded
innkeeper who briskly pops out with a helping of oats in
his hand; a tramp in worn shoes made of bast trudging
a distance of eight hundred *versts* [note this constant
fooling with figures—not five hundred and not a hundred
but eight hundred, for numbers themselves tend toward
an individuality of sorts in Gogol's creative atmosphere];
miserable little towns built anyhow with shabby shops
knocked together by means of a few boards, selling bar-
rels of flour, bast shoes [for the tramp who has just
passed], fancy breads and other trifles; striped barriers,
bridges under repair [i.e. *eternally* under repair—one of
the features of Gogol's straggling, drowsy, ramshackle
Russia]; a limitless expanse of grassland on both sides of
the road, the traveling coaches of country squires, a soldier on horseback dragging a green case with its load of
leaden peas and the legend: 'Battery such-and-such';
green, yellow and black bands [Gogol finds just the necessary space allowed by Russian syntax to insert "freshly
upturned" before "black," meaning stripes of newly

108

plowed earth] variegating the plains; a voice singing afar; crests of pines in the mist; the tolling of church bells dying away in the distance; crows like flies and the limitless horizon. . . . Rus! Rus! [ancient and poetic name for Russia] I see you, from my lovely enchanted remoteness I see you: a country of dinginess and bleakness and dispersal; no arrogant wonders of nature crowned by the arrogant wonders of art appear within you to delight or terrify the eyes: no cities with many-windowed tall palaces that have grown out of cliffs, no showy trees, no ivy that has grown out of walls amid the roar and eternal spray of waterfalls; one does not have to throw back one's head in order to contemplate some heavenly agglomeration of great rocks towering above the land [this is Gogol's private Russia, not the Russia of the Urals, the Altai, the Caucasus]. There are none of those dark archways with that tangle of vine, ivy and incalculable millions of roses, successive vistas through which one can suddenly glimpse afar the immortal outline of radiant mountains that leap into limpid silvery skies; all within you is open wilderness and level ground; your stunted towns that stick up among the plains are no more discernible than dots and signs [i.e. on a map]: nothing in you can charm and seduce the eye. So what is the incomprehensible secret force driving me towards you? Why do I constantly hear the echo of your mournful song as it is carried from sea to sea throughout your entire expanse? Tell me the secret of your song. What is this, calling and sobbing and plucking at my heart? What are these sounds that are both a stab and a kiss, why do they come rushing into my soul and fluttering about my heart? Rus! Tell me

109

what do you want of me! What is the strange bond secretly uniting us? Why do you look at me thus, and why has everything you contain turned upon me eyes full of expectancy? And while I stand thus, sorely perplexed and quite still, lo, a threatening cloud heavy with future rains comes over my head and my mind is mute before the greatness of your expanse. What does this unlimited space portend? And since you are without end yourself, is it not within you that a boundless thought will be born? And if a giant comes will it not happen there where there is room enough for the mightiest limbs and the mightiest stride? Your gigantic expanse grimly surrounds me and with a dreadful vividness is reflected in my depths; a supernatural power makes my eyes bright. . . . Oh, what a shining, splendid remoteness unknown to the world! Rus! . . .

" 'Stop, stop, you fool,' Chichikov was shouting at Selifan [which stresses the fact of this lyrical outburst's not being Chichikov's own meditation]. 'Wait till I give you a slap with my scabbard,' shouted a State Courier with yard long moustaches, . . . 'Damn your soul, don't you see that this is a governmental carriage?' And like a phantom the *troika* vanished with a thunder of wheels and a whirl of dust."

The remoteness of the poet from his country is transformed into the remoteness of Russia's future which Gogol somehow identifies with the future of his work, with the Second Part of *Dead Souls*, the book that everybody in Russia was expecting from him and that he was trying to make himself believe he would write. For me *Dead Souls* ends with Chichikov's departure from the town of N. I hardly know what to admire most when considering the following remarkable spurt of eloquence which brings the First Part to its close: the magic of its poetry—or magic of quite a different kind; for Gogol was faced by the double task of somehow having Chichikov escape just retribution by flight and of diverting the reader's attention from the still more uncomfortable fact that no retribution in terms of human law could overtake Satan's home-bound, hell-bound agent.

". . . Selifan added in a special singsong treble key something that sounded like 'Come, boys.' The horses perked up and had the light *britzka* speeding as if it were made of fluff. Selifan contented himself with waving his whip and emitting low guttural cries as he gently bounced up and down on his box while the *troika* either flew up a hillock or skimmed downhill again all along the undulating and slightly sloping highway. Chichikov did nothing but smile every time he was slightly thrown up on his leathern cushion, for he was a great lover of fast driving. And pray, find me the Russian who does not care for fast driving? Inclined as he is to let himself go, to whirl his life away and send it to the devil, his soul cannot but love speed. For is there not a kind of lofty and magic melody in fast driving? You seem to feel some unknown power lifting you up and placing you upon its wing, and then you are flying yourself and everything is flying by: the mileposts fly, merchants fly by on the boxes of their carriages, forests fly on both sides of the road in a dark succession of firs and pines together with the sound of hacking axes and the cries of crows; the entire highway is flying none knows whither away into the dissolving distance; and there is something frightening in this rapid

111

shimmer amid which passing and vanishing things do not have time to have their outlines fixed and only the sky above with fleecy clouds and a prying moon appears motionless. Oh *troika*, winged *troika*, tell me who invented you? Surely, nowhere but among a nimble nation could you have been born: in a country which has taken itself in earnest and has evenly spread far and wide over one half of the globe, so that once you start counting the milestones you may count on till a speckled haze dances before your eyes. And, methinks, there is nothing very tricky about a Russian carriage. No iron screws hold it together; its parts have been fitted and knocked into shape anyhow by means of an axe and a gauge and the acumen of a Yaroslav peasant; its driver does not wear any of your foreign jackboots; he consists of a beard and a pair of mittens, and he sits on a nondescript seat; but as soon as he strains up and throws back his whip-hand, and plunges into a wailing song, ah then—the steeds speed like the summer wind, the blurred wheelspokes form a circular void, the road gives a shiver, a passer-by stops short with an exclamation of fright—and lo, the *troika* has wings, wings, wings. . . . And now all you can see afar is a whirl of dust boring a hole in the air.

"Rus, are you not similar in your headlong motion to one of those nimble *troikas* that none can overtake? The flying road turns into smoke under you, bridges thunder and pass, all falls back and is left behind! The witness of your course stops as if struck by some divine miracle: is this not lightning that has dropped from the sky? And what does this awesome motion mean? What is the passing strange force contained in these passing strange

112

steeds? Steeds, steeds—what steeds! Has the whirlwind
a home in your manes? Is every sinew in you aglow with
a new sense of hearing? For as soon as the song you know
reaches you from above, you three, bronze-breasted,
strain as one, and then your hoofs hardly touch the
ground, and you are drawn out like three taut lines that
rip the air, and all is transfigured by the divine inspiration of speed! . . . Rus, whither are you speeding so?
Answer me. No answer. The middle bell trills out in a
dream its liquid soliloquy; the roaring air is torn to pieces
and becomes Wind; all things on earth fly by and other
nations and states gaze askance as they step aside and
give her the right of way."

Beautiful as all this final crescendo sounds, it is from
the stylistic point of view merely a conjuror's patter ena-
bling an object to disappear, the particular object being—
Chichikov.

4. THE TEACHER AND GUIDE

1

LEAVING RUSSIA AGAIN IN MAY 1842 GOGOL RESUMED HIS
weird wanderings abroad. Rolling wheels had spun for
him the yarn of the first part of *Dead Souls;* the circles he
had described himself on his first series of journeys
through a blurred Europe had resulted in round Chichikov becoming a revolving top, a dim rainbow; physical
gyration had assisted the author in hypnotizing himself
and his heroes into that kaleidoscopic nightmare which
for years to come simple souls were to accept as a "pano-
rama of Russia" (or "Homelife in Russia"). It was time
now to go into training for the Second Part.

One wonders whether at the back of his mind which
was so fantastically humped, Gogol did not assume that
rolling wheels, long roads unwinding themselves like
sympathetic serpents and the vaguely intoxicating quality of smooth steady motion which had proved so satis-

114

factory in the writing of the first part would automatically produce a second book which would form a clear luminous ring round the whirling colors of the first one. That it must be a halo, of this he was convinced; otherwise the first part might be deemed the magic of the Devil. In accordance with his system of laying the foundation for a book after he had published it he managed to convince himself that the (as yet unwritten) Second Part had actually given birth to the First and that the First would fatally remain merely an illustration bereft of its legend if the parent volume was not presented to a slow-witted public. In reality, he was to be hopelessly hampered by the autocratic form of the first part. When he attempted to compose the second, he was bound to act in much the same way as that murderer in one of Chesterton's stories who was forced to make all the note paper in his victim's house conform to the insolite shape of a fake suicide message.

Morbid wariness may have added certain other considerations. Passionately eager as he was to learn in detail what people thought of his work—any kind of person or critic, from the knave in the Government's pay to the fool fawning on public opinion—he had a hard time trying to explain to his correspondents that what merely interested him in critical reviews was a more extensive and objective view that they were giving him of his own self. It greatly bothered him to learn that earnest people were seeing in *Dead Souls*, with satisfaction or disgust, a spirited condemnation of slavery, just as they had seen an attack on corruption in *The Government Inspector*. For in the civic reader's mind *Dead Souls* was gently

115

NIKOLAI GOGOL

turning into *Uncle Tom's Cabin*. One doubts whether this
bothered him less than the attitude of those critics—
blackcoated worthies of the old school, pious spinsters
and Greek Orthodox puritans—who deplored the "sensu-
ousness" of his images. He was also acutely aware of the
power his artistic genius had over man and of the—loath-
some to him—responsibility that went with such power.
Something in him wanted a still greater sway (without the
responsibility) like the fisherman's wife in Pushkin's tale
who wanted a still bigger castle. Gogol became a preacher
because he needed a pulpit to explain the ethics of his
books and because a direct contact with readers seemed
to him to be the natural development of his own mag-
netic force. Religion gave him the necessary intonation
and method. It is doubtful whether it gave him anything
else.

2

A unique rolling stone, gathering—or thinking he
would gather—a unique kind of moss, he spent many
summers wandering from spa to spa. His complaint was
difficult to cure because it was both vague and variable:
attacks of melancholy when his mind would be benumbed
with unspeakable forebodings and nothing except an
abrupt change of surroundings could bring relief; or else
a recurrent state of physical distress marked by shiverings
when no abundance of clothing could warm his limbs and
when the only thing that helped, if persistently repeated,
was a brisk walk—the longer the better. The paradox was
that while needing constant movement to prompt inspiration, this movement physically prevented him from writ-

116

ing. Still, the winters spent in Italy, in comparative comfort, were even less productive than those fitful stage coach periods. Dresden, Badgastein, Salzburg, Munich, Venice, Florence, Rome, Florence, Mantua, Verona, Innsbruck, Salzburg, Karlsbad, Prague, Greifenberg, Berlin, Badgastein, Prague, Salzburg, Venice, Bologna, Florence, Rome, Nice, Paris, Frankfurt, Dresden,—and all over again, this series with its repetition of names of grand tour towns is not really the itinerary of a man seeking health—or collecting hotel labels to show in Moscow, Ohio or Moscow, Russia—but merely the dotted line of a vicious circle with no geographical meaning. Gogol's spas were not really spatial. Central Europe for him was but an optical phenomenon—and the only thing that really mattered, the only real obsession, the only real tragedy was that his creative power kept steadily and hopelessly ebbing away. When Tolstoy surrendered the writing of novels to the ethical, mystical and educational urge, his genius was ripe and ruddy, and the fragments of imaginative work posthumously published show that his art was still developing after Anna Karenina's death. But Gogol was a man of few books and the plans he had made to write the book of his life happened to coincide with the beginning of his decline as a writer—after he had reached the summits of *The Government Inspector*, *The Overcoat* and the first volume of *Dead Souls*.

3

The period of preaching begins with certain last touches that he put to *Dead Souls*—those strange hints at a prodigious apotheosis in the future. A peculiar biblical accent swells the contours of his sentences in the numerous letters he writes to his friends from abroad. "Woe to those who do not heed my word! Leave all things for a while, leave all such pleasures that tickle your fancy at idle moments. Obey me: during one year, one year only, attend to the affairs of your country estate." Sending landowners back to face the problems of country life (with all the contemporary implications of the business— unsatisfactory crops, disreputable overseers, unmanageable slaves, idleness, theft, poverty, lack of economic and "spiritual" organization) becomes his main theme and command—a command couched in the tones of a prophet ordering men to discard all earthly riches. But, despite the tone, Gogol was ordering landowners to do exactly the opposite (although it did sound like some great sacrifice that he was demanding from his bleak hilltop, in the name of God): leave the great town where you are frittering away your precarious income and return to the lands that God gave you for the express purpose that you might grow as rich as the black earth itself, with robust and cheerful peasants gratefully toiling under your fatherly supervision. "The landowners' business is divine"— this was the gist of Gogol's sermon.

One cannot help noting how eager, how overeager he was not only to have those sulky landowners and disgruntled officials return to their provincial offices, to their lands and crops, but also to have them give him a minute account of their impressions. One almost might suppose that there was something else at the back of Gogol's mind, that Pandora's box mind, something more important to him than the ethical and economic conditions of life in rural Russia; namely—a pathetic attempt to obtain "authentic" first-hand material for his book; because he was in the worst plight that a writer can be in: he had lost the gift of imagining facts and believed that facts may exist by themselves.

The trouble is that bare facts do not exist in a state of nature, for they are never really quite bare: the white trace of a wrist watch, a curled piece of sticking plaster on a bruised heel, these cannot be discarded by the most ardent nudist. A mere string of figures will disclose the identity of the stringer as neatly as tame ciphers yielded their treasure to Poe. The crudest *curriculum vitae* crows and flaps its wings in a style peculiar to the undersigner. I doubt whether you can even give your telephone number without giving something of yourself. But Gogol in spite of all the things he said about wishing to know mankind because he loved mankind, was really not much interested in the personality of the giver. He wanted his facts absolutely bare—and at the same time he demanded not mere strings of figures but a complete set of minute observations. When some of his more indulgent friends yielded reluctantly to his requests and then warmed up to the business and sent him accounts of provincial and rural affairs—they would get from him a howl of disappointment and dismay instead of thanks; for his correspondents were not Gogols. They had been ordered by him to describe things—just describe them. They did so with a vengeance. Gogol was balked of his material because his friends were not writers whereas he could not address himself to those friends of his who were writers, because then the facts supplied would be anything but bare. The whole business is indeed one of the best illustrations of the utter stupidity of such terms as "bare facts" and "realism." Gogol—a "realist"! There are text books that say so. And very possibly Gogol himself in his pathetic and futile efforts to get the bits that would form the mosaic of his book from his readers themselves, surmised that he was acting in a throughly rational way. It is so simple, he kept on peevishly repeating to various ladies and gentlemen, just sit down for an hour every day and jot down all you see and hear. He might as well have told them to mail him the moon—no matter in what quarter. And never mind if a star or two and a streak of mist get mixed up with it in your hastily tied blue paper parcel. And if a horn gets broken, I will replace it.

His biographers have been rather puzzled by the irritation he showed at not getting what he wanted. They were puzzled by the singular fact that a writer of genius was surprised at other people not being able to write as well as he did. In reality what made Gogol so cross was that the subtle method he had devised of getting material, which he could no longer create himself, did not work. The growing conscience of his impotence became a kind of disease which he concealed from himself and from others. He welcomed interruptions and obstacles ("obstacles are our wings" as he put it) because they could be held responsible for the delay. The whole philosophy of his later years with such basic notions as "the darker your heavens the more radiant tomorrow's blessing will be" was prompted by the constant feeling that this morrow would never come.

On the other hand, he would fly into a terrific passion if anybody suggested that the coming of the blessing might be hastened—I am not a hack, not a journeyman, not a journalist—he would write. And while he did all he could to make himself and others believe that he was going to produce a book of the utmost importance to Russia (and "Russia" was now synonymous with "humanity" in his very Russian mind) he refused to tolerate rumors which he engendered himself by his mystical innuendoes. The period of his life following upon the First Part of *Dead Souls* may be entitled "Great Expectations"—from the reader's point of view at least. Some were expecting a still more definite and vigorous indictment of corruption and social injustice, others were looking forward to a rollicking yarn with a good laugh on every page. While Gogol was shivering in one of those stone cold rooms that you find only in the extreme South of Europe, and was assuring his friends that henceforth his life was sacred, that his bodily form must be handled with care and loved and nursed as the cracked earthen jar containing that wine of wisdom, (i.e. the Second Part of *Dead Souls*), the glad news was spread at home that Gogol was completing a book dealing with the adventures of a Russian general in Rome—the funniest book he had ever written. The tragical part of the business was that as a matter of fact the best thing in the remnants of the second volume that have reached us happens to be the passages relating to that farcical automaton, General Betrishchev.

4

Rome and Russia formed a combination of a deeper kind in Gogol's unreal world. Rome was to him a place where he had spells of physical fitness that the North denied him. The flowers of Italy (of which flowers he said: "I *respect* flowers that have grown by themselves on a grave") filled him with a fierce desire to be changed into a Nose: to lack everything else such as eyes, arms, legs, and to be nothing but one huge Nose, "with nostrils the size of two goodly pails so that I might inhale all possible vernal perfumes." He was especially nose-conscious when living in Italy. There was also that special Italian sky "all silvery and shot with a satiny gloss but disclosing the deepest tone of blue when viewed through the arches of the Coliseum." Seeking a kind of relaxation from his own distorted and dreadful and devilish image of the world he pathetically endeavored to cling to the normality of a second rate painter's conception of Rome as an essentially "picturesque" place: "I like the donkeys too—the donkeys that amble or jog at full speed with half closed eyes and picturesquely carry upon their back strong stately Italian women whose white caps remain brightly visible as they recede; or when these donkeys drag along, in a less picturesque way, with difficulty and many a stumble, some lank stiff Englishman who sports a greenish brown waterproof mackintosh [literal translation] and screws up his legs so as to avoid scraping the ground; or when a bloused painter rides by complete with van Dyke beard and wooden paintbox" etc. He could not keep up this kind of style for long and the conventional novel

122

about the adventures of an Italian gentleman that at one time he contemplated writing happily remained limited to a few lurid generalizations "Everything in her from her shoulders to her *antique breathing* leg and to the *last toe* of her foot is the crown of creation"—no, enough of that, or the hemmings and hawings of a wistful provincial clerk musing his misery away in the depths of Gogolian Russia will get hopelessly mixed up with classical eloquence.

5

Then there was Ivanov in Rome, the great Russian painter. For more than twenty years he worked at his picture "The Appearance of the Messiah to the People." His destiny was in many respects similar to that of Gogol with the difference that at last Ivanov *did* finish his masterpiece: the story is told that when it was finally exhibited (in 1858) he calmly sat there putting a few final touches to it—this after twenty years of work!—quite unconcerned by the crowd in the exhibition hall. Both Ivanov and Gogol lived in permanent poverty because neither could tear himself away from his life work in order to earn a living; both were constantly pestered by impatient people rebuking them for their slowness; both were highstrung, ill-tempered, uneducated, and ridiculously clumsy in all worldly matters. In his capital description of Ivanov's work Gogol stresses this relationship, and one cannot help feeling that when he spoke of the chief figure in the picture ("And He, in heavenly peace and divine remoteness, is already nearing with quick firm steps" . . .), Ivanov's picture got somehow mixed in his thoughts with the religious element of his own still unwritten book which he saw steadily approaching from the silvery Italian heights.

6

The letters he wrote to his friends while working on *Selected Passages from Correspondence with Friends* did not include these passages (if they had, Gogol would not have been Gogol), but they much resemble them both in matter and tone. He thought some of them so inspired from above that he requested their being read "daily during the week of Fast"; it is doubtful however whether any of his correspondents were sufficiently meek to do this—to summon the members of their household and selfconsciously clear their throats—rather like the Mayor about to read the all-important letter in Act I of *The Government Inspector*. The language of these epistles is almost a parody of sanctimonious intonation but there are some beautiful interruptions, as when, for instance, Gogol uses some very strong and worldly language in regard to a printing house which had swindled him. The pious actions which he plans out for his friends come to coincide with more or less bothersome commissions. He developed a most extraordinary system of laying penance on "sinners" by making them slave for him—running errands, buying and packing the books he needed, copying out critical reviews, haggling with printers, etc. In compensation he would send a copy of, say, *The Imitation of Jesus Christ* with detailed instructions telling how to use it—and quite similar instructions occur in passages concerning hydrotherapy and digestive troubles—"Two

124

glasses of cold water before breakfast" is the tip he gives a fellow sufferer.

"Set aside all your affairs and busy yourself with my own"—this is the general trend—which of course would have been quite logical had his correspondents been disciples firmly believing that "he who helps Gogol helps God." But the real people who got these letters from Rome, Dresden or Baden-Baden decided that Gogol was either going mad or that he was deliberately playing the fool. Perhaps he was not too scrupulous in using his divine rights. He put his comfortable situation as God's representative to very personal ends as, for instance, when giving a piece of his mind to persons who had offended him in the past. When the critic Pogodin's wife died and the man was frantic with grief, this is what Gogol wrote him: "Jesus Christ will help you to become a gentleman, which you are neither by education nor inclination—she is speaking through me."—a letter absolutely unique in the correspondence of compassion. Aksakov was one of the few people who decided at last to let Gogol know his reaction to certain admonishments. "Dear Friend," he wrote, "I never doubt the sincerity of your beliefs or your good will in respect to your friends; but I frankly confess being annoyed by the form your beliefs take. Even more —they frighten me. I am 53 years old. I read Thomas à Kempis before you were born. I am as far from condemning the beliefs of others as I am from accepting them— whereas you come and tell me as if I were a schoolboy— and without having the vaguest notion of what my own ideas are—to read the *Imitation*—and moreover, to do so at certain fixed hours after my morning coffee, a chapter

125

a day, like a lesson. . . . This is both ridiculous and aggravating. . . ."

But Gogol persisted in his newly found *genre*. He maintained that whatever he said or did was inspired by the same spirit that would presently disclose its mysterious essence in the second and third volumes of *Dead Souls*. He also maintained that the volume of *Selected Passages* was meant as a test, as a means of putting the reader into a suitable frame of mind for the reception of the sequel to *Dead Souls*. One is forced to assume that he utterly failed to realize the exact nature of the stepping stone he was so kindly providing.

The main body of the *Passages* consists of Gogol's advice to Russian landowners, provincial officials and, generally, Christians. County squires are regarded as the agents of God, hard working agents holding shares in paradise and getting more or less substantial commissions in earthly currency. "Gather all your *mouzhiks* and tell them that you make them labor because this is what God intended them to do—not at all because you need money for your pleasures; and at this point take out a banknote and in visual proof of your words burn it before their eyes. . . ." The image is pleasing: the squire standing on his porch and demonstrating a crisp, delicately tinted banknote with the deliberate gestures of a professional magician; a Bible is prepared on an innocent-looking table; a boy holds a lighted candle; the audience of bearded peasants gapes in respectful suspense; there is a murmur of awe as the banknote turns into a butterfly of fire; the conjuror lightly and briskly rubs his hands—just the inside of the fingers; then after some patter he opens the Bible and lo, Phoenix-like, the treasure is there.

The censor rather generously left out this passage in the first edition as implying a certain disrespect for the Government by the wanton destruction of state money— much in the same way as the worthies in *The Government Inspector* condemned the breaking of state property (namely chairs) at the hands of violent professors of ancient history. One is tempted to continue this simile and say that in a sense Gogol in those *Selected Passages* seemed to be impersonating one of his own delightfully grotesque characters. No schools, no books, just you and the village priest—this is the educational system he suggests to the squire. "The peasant must not even *know* that there exist other books besides the Bible." "Take the village priest with you everywhere. . . . Make him your estate manager." Samples of robust curses to be employed whenever a lazy serf is to be pricked to the quick are supplied in another astounding passage. There are also some grand bursts of irrelevant rhetoric—and a vicious thrust at the unlucky Pogodin. We find such things as "every man has become a rotten rag" or "compatriots, I am frightened"—the "compatriots" ("saw-awe-tea-chesstven-nikee") pronounced with the intonation of "comrades" or "brethren"—only more so.

The book provoked a tremendous row. Public opinion in Russia was essentially democratic—and, incidentally, deeply admired America. No Tsar could break this backbone (it was snapped only much later by the Soviet regime). There were several schools of civic thought in the middle of last century; and though the most radical one was to degenerate later into the atrocious dullness of Populism, Marxism, Internationalism and what not (then to spin on and complete its inevitable circle with State Serfdom and Reactionary Nationalism), there can be no doubt whatever that in Gogol's time the "Westerners" formed a cultural power vastly exceeding in scope and quality anything that reactionary fogeys could think up. Thus it would not be quite fair to view the critic Belinsky, for instance, as merely a forerunner (which phylogenetically he of course was) of those writers of the Sixties and Seventies who virulently enforced the supremacy of civic values over artistic ones; what they meant by "artistic" is another question: Chernyshevski or Pissarev would solemnly accumulate reasons to prove that writing textbooks for the people was more important than painting "marble pillars and nymphs"—which they thought was "pure art." Incidentally this outdated method of bringing all esthetic possibilities to the level of one's own little conceptions and capacities in the water color line when criticizing "art for art" from a national, political or generally philistine point of view, is very amusing in the argumentation of some modern American critics. Whatever his naive shortcomings as an appraiser of artistic values, Belinsky had as a citizen and as a thinker that wonderful instinct for truth and freedom which only party politics can destroy—and party politics were still in their infancy. At the time his cup still contained a pure liquid; with the help of Dobrolyubov and Pissarev and Mikhailovsky it was doomed to turn into a breeding fluid for most sinister germs. On the other hand Gogol was obviously stuck in the mud and had mistaken the oily glaze on a filthy puddle for a mystic rainbow of sorts. Belinsky's famous letter, ripping up as it does the *Selected Passages* ("this inflated and sluttish hullaballoo of words and phrases") is a noble document. It contained too a spirited attack on Tsardom so that distribution of copies of the "Belinsky letter" soon became punishable by Hard Labor in Siberia. Gogol, it seems, was mainly upset by Belinsky's hints at his fawning upon aristocrats for the sake of financial assistance. Belinsky, of course, belonged to the "poor and proud" school; Gogol as a Christian condemned "pride."

In spite of the torrents of abuse, complaints and sarcasm that flooded his book from most quarters, Gogol kept a rather brave countenance. Although admitting that the book had been written "in a morbid and constrained state of mind" and that "inexperience in the art of such writing had, with the Devil's help, transformed the humility I actually felt into an arrogant display of self-sufficiency" (or, as he puts it elsewhere, "I let myself go like a regular Khlestakov"), he maintained with the solemnity of a staunch martyr that his book was necessary, and this for three reasons: it had made people show him what he was; it had shown him and themselves what *they* were; and it had cleansed the general atmosphere as efficiently as a thunderstorm. This was about equal to saying that he had done what he had intended to do: prepare public opinion for the reception of the Second Part of *Dead Souls*.

7

During his long years abroad and hectic visits to Russia Gogol kept jotting down on scraps of paper (in his carriage, at some inn, in a friend's house, anywhere) odds

and ends relating to the supreme masterpiece. At times he
would have quite a series of chapters which he would
read to his most intimate friends in great secret; at others
he would have nothing; sometimes a friend would be
copying pages and pages of it and sometimes Gogol insisted that not a word had been penned yet—everything
was in his brain. Apparently there were several minor
holocausts preceding the main one just before his death.

At a certain point of his tragic efforts he did something
which, in view of his physical frailty, was rather in the
nature of a feat: he journeyed to Jerusalem with the object of obtaining what he needed for the writing of his
book—divine advice, strength and creative fancy—much
in the same fashion as a sterile woman might beg the Vir-
gin for a child in the painted darkness of a medieval
church. For several years, however, he kept postponing
this pilgrimage: his spirit, he said, was not ready; God did
not wish it yet: "mark the obstacles he puts in my way"; a
certain state of mind (vaguely resembling the Catholic
"grace") had to come into being so as to ensure a maxi-
mum probability of success in his (absolutely pagan) en-
terprise; moreover, he needed a reliable traveling companion who would not be a bore; would be silent or
talkative at moments exactly synchronizing with the pilgrim's prismatic mood; and who, when required, would
tuck in the traveling rug with a soothing hand. When at
last in January, 1848, he launched upon his hazardous en-
terprise, there was just as little reason for its not turning
into a dismal flop as there ever had been.

A sweet old lady, Nadezhda Nikolayevna Sheremetev,
one of Gogol's truest and dullest correspondents, with

whom he had exchanged many a prayer for the welfare of his soul, saw him to the town barrier beyond Moscow. Gogol's papers were probably in perfect order but somehow or other he disliked the idea of their being examined, and the holy pilgrimage began with one of those morbid mystifications which he was wont to practice on policemen. Unfortunately, it involved the old lady too. At the barrier she embraced the pilgrim, broke into tears and made the sign of the cross over Gogol who responded effusively. At this moment papers were asked for: an official wanted to know who exactly was leaving. "This little old lady," cried Gogol, and rolled away in his carriage, leaving Madame Sheremetev in a very awkward position.

To his mother he sent a special prayer to be read in church by the local priest. In this prayer he begged the Lord to save him from robbers in the East and to spare him seasickness during the crossing. The Lord ignored the second request: between Naples and Malta, on the capricious ship "Capri," Gogol vomited so horribly that "the passengers marveled greatly." The rest of the pilgrimage was singularly dim so that had there not been some official proof of its actual occurrence one might easily suppose that he invented the whole journey as he had formerly invented an excursion to Spain. When for years on end you have been telling people that you are going to do something and when you are sick of not being able to make up your mind, it saves a good deal of trouble to have them believe one fine day that you have done it already—and what a relief to be able to drop the matter.

"What can my dreamlike impressions convey to you? I saw the Holy Land through the mist of a dream." (From a letter to Zhukovsky). We have a glimpse of him quarreling in the desert with Basilli, his traveling companion. Somewhere in Samaria he plucked an asphodel, somewhere in Galilee a poppy (having a vague inclination for botany as Rousseau had). It rained at Nazareth, and he sought shelter, and was stranded there for a couple of hours "hardly realizing that I was in Nazareth as I sat there" (on a bench under which a hen had taken refuge) "just as I would have been sitting at some stage-coach station somewhere in Russia." The sanctuaries he visited failed to fuse with their mystic reality in his soul. In result, the Holy Land did as little for his soul (and his book) as German sanatoriums had done for his body.

8

During the last ten years of his life, Gogol kept stubbornly brooding over the sequel to *Dead Souls*. He had lost the magic capacity of creating life out of nothing; his imagination needed some ready material to work upon for he still had the strength of repeating himself; although unable to produce a brand new world as he had done in the First Part, he thought he could use the same texture and recombine its designs in another fashion, namely: in conformity with a definite purpose which had been absent from the First Part, but which was now supposed not only to provide a new driving force, but also to endow the First Part with a retrospective meaning.

Apart from the special character of Gogol's case, the

general delusion into which he had lapsed was of course disastrous. A writer is lost when he grows interested in such questions as "what is art?" and "what is an artist's duty?" Gogol decided that the purpose of literary art was to cure ailing souls by producing in them a sense of harmony and peace. The treatment was also to include a strong dose of didactic medicine. He proposed to portray national defects and national virtues in such a manner as to help readers to persevere in the latter and rid themselves of the former. At the beginning of his work on the sequel his intention was to make his characters not "wholly virtuous," but "more important" than those of Part One. To use the pretty slang of publishers and reviewers he wished to invest them with more "human appeal." Writing novels was merely a sinful game if the author's "sympathetic attitude" towards some of his characters and a "critical attitude" towards others, was not disclosed with perfect clarity. So clearly, in fact, that even the humblest reader (who likes books in dialogue form with a minimum of "descriptions"—because conversations are "life") would know whose side to take. What Gogol promised to give the reader—or rather the readers he imagined —were facts. He would, he said, represent Russians not by the "petty traits" of individual freaks, not by "smug vulgarities and oddities," not through the sacrilegious medium of a lone artist's private vision, but in such a manner that "the Russian would appear in the fullness of his national nature, in all the rich variety of the inner forces contained in him." In other words the "dead souls" would become "live souls."

It is evident that what Gogol (or any other writer having similar unfortunate intentions) is saying here can be reduced to much simpler terms: "I have imagined one kind of world in my First Part, but now I am going to imagine another kind which will conform better to what I imagine are the concepts of Right and Wrong more or less consciously shared by my imaginary readers." Success in such cases (with popular magazine novelists, etc.) is directly dependent on how closely the author's vision of "readers" corresponds to the traditional, i.e. imaginary, notions that readers have of their own selves, notions carefully bred and sustained by a regular supply of mental chewing gum provided by the corresponding publishers. But Gogol's position was of course not so simple, first because what he proposed to write was to be on the lines of a religious revelation, and second, because the imaginary reader was supposed not merely to enjoy sundry details of the revelation but to be morally helped, improved or even totally regenerated by the general effect of the book. The main difficulty lay in having to combine the material of the First Part, which from a philistine's viewpoint dealt with "oddities" (but which Gogol *had to* use since he no longer could create a new texture), with the kind of solemn sermon, staggering samples of which he had given in the *Selected Passages*. Although his first intention was to have his characters not "wholly virtuous" but "important" in the sense of their fully representing a rich mixture of Russian passions, moods and ideals, he gradually discovered that these "important" characters coming from under his pen were being adul-

134

terated by the inevitable oddities that they borrowed
from their natural medium and from their inner affinity
with the nightmare squires of the initial set. Consequently
the only way out was to have another alien group of characters which would be quite obviously and quite narrowly
"good" because any attempt at rich characterization in
their case would be bound to lead to the same weird
forms which the not "wholly virtuous" ones kept assum-
ing owing to their unfortunate ancestry.

When in 1847 Father Matthew, a fanatical Russian
priest who combined the eloquence of John Chrysos-
tom with the murkiest fads of the Dark Ages, begged
Gogol to give up literature altogether and busy himself
with devotional duties, such as preparing his soul for the
Other World as mapped by Father Matthew and such
like Fathers—Gogol did his best to make his correspond-
ent see how very good the good characters of *Dead Souls*
would be if only he was allowed by the Church to yield
to that urge for writing which God had instilled in him
behind Father Matthew's back: "Cannot an author present, in the frame of an attractive story, vivid examples
of human beings that are better men than those presented
by other writers? Examples are stronger than argumenta-
tions; before giving such examples all a writer needs is
to become a good man himself and lead the kind of life
that would please God. I would never have dreamt of
writing at all had there not been nowadays such a widespread reading of various novels and short stories, most
of which are immoral and sinfully alluring, but which are
read because they hold one's interest and are not devoid

of talent. I too have talent—the knack of making nature and men live in my tales; and since this is so, must I not present in the same attractive fashion righteous and pious people living according to the Divine Law? I want to tell you frankly that this, and not money or fame, is my main incentive for writing."

It would be of course ridiculous to suppose that Gogol spent ten years merely in trying to write something that would please the Church. What he was really trying to do was to write something that would please both Gogol the artist and Gogol the monk. He was obsessed by the thought that great Italian painters had done this again and again: a cool cloister, roses climbing a wall, a gaunt man wearing a skull-cap, the radiant fresh colors of the fresco he is working upon—these formed the professional setting which Gogol craved. Transmuted into literature, the completed *Dead Souls* was to form three connected images: Crime, Punishment and Redemption. The attainment of this object was absolutely impossible not only because Gogol's unique genius was sure to play havoc with any conventional scheme if given a free hand, but because he had forced the main role, that of the sinner, upon a person—if Chichikov can be called a person—who was most ridiculously unfit for that part and who moreover moved in a world where such things as saving one's soul simply did not happen. A sympathetically pictured priest in the midst of the Gogolian characters of the first volume would have been as utterly impossible as a *gauloiserie* in Pascal or a quotation from Thoreau in Stalin's latest speech.

In the few chapters of the Second Part that have been

preserved, Gogol's magic glasses become blurred. Chichikov though remaining (with a vengeance) in the center of the field somehow departs from the focal plane. There are several splendid passages in these chapters, but they are mere echoes of the First Part. And when the "good" characters appear—the thrifty landowner, the saintly merchant, the God-like Prince, one has the impression of perfect strangers crowding in to take possession of a draughty house where familiar things stand in dismal disorder. As I have already mentioned, Chichikov's swindles are but the phantoms and parodies of crime, so that no "real" retribution is possible without a distortion of the whole idea. The "good people" are false because they do not belong to Gogol's world and thus every contact between them and Chichikov is jarring and depressing. If Gogol did write the redemption part with a "good priest" (of a slightly Catholic type) saving Chichikov's soul in the depths of Siberia (there exist some scraps of information that Gogol studied Pallas' *Siberian Flora* in order to get the right background), and if Chichikov was fated to end his days as an emaciated monk in a remote monastery, then no wonder that the artist, in a last blinding flash of artistic truth, burnt the end of *Dead Souls*. Father Matthew could be satisfied that Gogol shortly before dying had renounced literature; but the brief blaze that might be deemed a proof and symbol of this renunciation happened to be exactly the opposite thing: as he crouched and sobbed in front of that stove ("Where?" queries my publisher. In Moscow.), an artist was destroying the labor of long years because he finally realized that the completed book was untrue to his gen-

137

ius; so Chichikov, instead of piously petering out in a
wooden chapel among ascetic fir trees on the shore of a
legendary lake, was restored to his native element; the
little blue flames of a humble hell.

5. THE APOTHEOSIS OF A MASK

1

". . . A CERTAIN MAN WHO WAS, I DARESAY, NOT VERY RE-markable: short he was and somewhat poxmarked and somewhat on the carroty side, and somewhat even blear-eyed and a little bald in front, with symmetrically wrin-kled cheeks and the kind of complexion termed hemor-rhoidal . . .

". . . His name was Bashmachkin. Already the name itself clearly shows that it had formerly come from *bash-mak*—a shoe. But when, and at what time had it come from "shoe," this is totally unknown. All of them—the fa-ther and the grandfather, and even the brother-in-law—absolutely all the Bashmachkins—used to wear boots which they resoled not more often than three times a year."

2

Gogol was a strange creature, but genius is always strange; it is only your healthy second-rater who seems to the grateful reader to be a wise old friend, nicely developing the reader's own notions of life. Great literature skirts the irrational. *Hamlet* is the wild dream of a neurotic scholar. Gogol's *The Overcoat* is a grotesque and grim nightmare making black holes in the dim pattern of life. The superficial reader of that story will merely see in it the heavy frolics of an extravagant buffoon; the solemn reader will take for granted that Gogol's prime intention was to denounce the horrors of Russian bureaucracy. But neither the person who wants a good laugh, nor the person who craves for books "that make one think" will understand what *The Overcoat* is really about. Give me the creative reader; this is a tale for him.

Steady Pushkin, matter-of-fact Tolstoy, restrained Chekhov have all had their moments of irrational insight which simultaneously blurred the sentence and disclosed a secret meaning worth the sudden focal shift. But with Gogol this shifting is the very basis of his art, so that whenever he tried to write in the round hand of literary tradition and to treat rational ideas in a logical way, he lost all trace of talent. When, as in his immortal *The Overcoat*, he really let himself go and pottered happily on the brink of his private abyss, he became the greatest artist that Russia has yet produced.

The sudden slanting of the rational plane of life may be accomplished of course in many ways, and every great writer has his own method. With Gogol it was a combina-

140

tion of two movements: a jerk and a glide. Imagine a trap-door that opens under your feet with absurd suddenness, and a lyrical gust that sweeps you up and then lets you fall with a bump into the next traphole. The absurd was Gogol's favorite muse—but when I say "the absurd," I do not mean the quaint or the comic. The absurd has as many shades and degrees as the tragic has, and moreover, in Gogol's case, it borders upon the latter. It would be wrong to assert that Gogol placed his characters in absurd situations. You cannot place a man in an absurd situation if the whole world he lives in is absurd; you cannot do this if you mean by "absurd" something provoking a chuckle or a shrug. But if you mean the pathetic, the human condition, if you mean all such things that in less weird worlds are linked up with the loftiest aspirations, the deepest sufferings, the strongest passions—then of course the necessary breach is there, and a pathetic human, lost in the midst of Gogol's nightmarish, irresponsible world would be "absurd," by a kind of secondary contrast.

On the lid of the tailor's snuff-box there was "the portrait of a General; I do not know what general because the tailor's thumb had made a hole in the general's face and a square of paper had been gummed over the hole." Thus with the absurdity of Akaky Akakyevich Bashmachkin. We did not expect that, amid the whirling masks, one mask would turn out to be a real face, or at least the place where that face ought to be. The essence of mankind is irrationally derived from the chaos of fakes which form Gogol's world. Akaky Akakyevich, the hero of *The Overcoat*, is absurd *because* he is pathetic, *because* he is human and *because* he has been engendered by those

141

very forces which seem to be in such contrast to him.

He is not merely human and pathetic. He is something more, just as the background is not mere burlesque. Somewhere behind the obvious contrast there is a subtle genetic link. His being discloses the same quiver and shimmer as does the dream world to which he belongs. The allusions to something else behind the crudely painted screens, are so artistically combined with the superficial texture of the narration that civic-minded Russians have missed them completely. But a creative reading of Gogol's story reveals that here and there in the most innocent descriptive passage, this or that word, sometimes a mere adverb or a preposition, for instance the word "even" or "almost," is inserted in such a way as to make the harmless sentence explode in a wild display of nightmare fireworks; or else the passage that had started in a rambling colloquial manner all of a sudden leaves the tracks and swerves into the irrational where it really belongs; or again, quite as suddenly, a door bursts open and a mighty wave of foaming poetry rushes in only to dissolve in bathos, or to turn into its own parody, or to be checked by the sentence breaking and reverting to a conjuror's patter, that patter which is such a feature of Gogol's style. It gives one the sensation of something ludicrous and at the same time stellar, lurking constantly around the corner—and one likes to recall that the difference between the comic side of things, and their cosmic side, depends upon one sibilant.

3

So what is that queer world, glimpses of which we keep catching through the gaps of the harmless looking sentences? It is in a way the *real* one but it looks wildly absurd to us, accustomed as we are to the stage setting that screens it. It is from these glimpses that the main character of *The Overcoat*, the meek little clerk, is formed, so that he embodies the spirit of that secret but real world which breaks through Gogol's style. He is, that meek little clerk, a ghost, a visitor from some tragic depths who by chance happened to assume the disguise of a petty official. Russian progressive critics sensed in him the image of the underdog and the whole story impressed them as a social protest. But it is something much more than that. The gaps and black holes in the texture of Gogol's style imply flaws in the texture of life itself. Something is very wrong and all men are mild lunatics engaged in pursuits that seem to them very important while an absurdly logical force keeps them at their futile jobs—this is the real "message" of the story. In this world of utter futility, of futile humility and futile domination, the highest degree that passion, desire, creative urge can attain is a new cloak which both tailors and customers adore on their knees. I am not speaking of the moral point or the moral

143

lesson. There can be no moral lesson in such a world because there are no pupils and no teachers: this world *is* and it excludes everything that might destroy it, so that any improvement, any struggle, any moral purpose or endeavor, are as utterly impossible as changing the course of a star. It is Gogol's world and as such wholly different from Tolstoy's world, or Pushkin's, or Chekhov's or my own. But after reading Gogol one's eyes may become gogolized and one is apt to see bits of his world in the most unexpected places. I have visited many countries, and something like Akaky Akakyevich's overcoat has been the passionate dream of this or that chance acquaintance who never had heard about Gogol.

4

The plot of *The Overcoat* * is very simple. A poor little clerk makes a great decision and orders a new overcoat. The coat while in the making becomes the dream of his life. On the very first night that he wears it he is robbed of it on a dark street. He dies of grief and his ghost haunts the city. This is all in the way of plot, but of course the *real* plot (as always with Gogol) lies in the style, in the inner structure of this transcendental anecdote. In order to appreciate it at its true worth one must perform a kind of mental somersault so as to get rid of conventional values in literature and follow the author along the dream road of his superhuman imagination. Gogol's world is somewhat related to such conceptions of modern physics as the "Concertina Universe" or the "Explosion Universe"; it is

* The *shinel* (from chenille) of the Russian title is a deep-caped, ample-sleeved furred carrick.

far removed from the comfortably revolving clockwork worlds of the last century. There is a curvature in literary style as there is curvature in space,—but few are the Russian readers who do care to plunge into Gogol's magic chaos head first, with no restraint or regret. The Russian who thinks Turgenev was a great writer, and bases his notion of Pushkin upon Chaïkovsky's vile libretti, will merely paddle into the gentlest wavelets of Gogol's mysterious sea and limit his reaction to an enjoyment of what he takes to be whimsical humor and colorful quips. But the diver, the seeker for black pearls, the man who prefers the monsters of the deep to the sunshades on the beach, will find in *The Overcoat* shadows linking our state of existence to those other states and modes which we dimly apprehend in our rare moments of irrational perception. The prose of Pushkin is three-dimensional; that of Gogol is four-dimensional, at least. He may be compared to his contemporary, the mathematician Lobachevsky, who blasted Euclid and discovered a century ago many of the theories which Einstein later developed. If parallel lines do not meet it is not because meet they cannot, but because they have other things to do. Gogol's art as disclosed in *The Overcoat* suggests that parallel lines not only may meet, but that they can wriggle and get most extravagantly entangled, just as two pillars reflected in water indulge in the most wobbly contortions if the necessary ripple is there. Gogol's genius is exactly that ripple—two and two make five, if not the square root of five, and it all happens quite naturally in Gogol's world, where neither rational mathematics nor indeed any of our pseudophysical agreements with ourselves can be seriously said to exist.

145

5

The clothing process indulged in by Akaky Akakyevich, the making and the putting on of the cloak, is really his *disrobing* and his gradual reversion to the stark nakedness of his own ghost. From the very beginning of the story he is in training for his supernaturally high jump— and such harmless looking details as his tiptoeing in the streets to spare his shoes or his not quite knowing whether he is in the middle of the street or in the middle of the sentence, these details gradually dissolve the clerk Akaky Akakyevich so that towards the end of the story his ghost seems to be the most tangible, the most real part of his being. The account of his ghost haunting the streets of St. Petersburg in search of the cloak of which he had been robbed and finally appropriating that of a high official who had refused to help him in his misfortune—this account, which to the unsophisticated may look like an ordinary ghost story, is transformed towards the end into something for which I can find no precise epithet. It is both an apotheosis and a *dégringolade*. Here it is:

"The Important Person almost died of fright. In his office and generally in the presence of subordinates he was a man of strong character, and whoever glanced at his manly appearance and shape used to imagine his kind of temper with something of a shudder; at the present moment however he (as happens in the case of many people of prodigiously powerful appearance) experienced such terror that, not without reason, he *even* expected to have a fit of some sort. He *even* threw off his cloak of his own accord and then exhorted the coachman

146

in a wild voice to take him home and drive like mad. Upon hearing tones which were generally used at critical moments and were *even* [notice the recurrent use of this word] accompanied by something far more effective, the coachman thought it wiser to draw his head in; he lashed at the horses, and the carriage sped like an arrow. Six minutes later, or a little more, [according to Gogol's special timepiece] the Important Person was already at the porch of his house. Pale, frightened and cloakless, instead of arriving at Caroline Ivanovna's [a woman he kept] he had thus come home; he staggered to his bedroom and spent an exceedingly troubled night, so that next morning, at breakfast, his daughter said to him straightaway: 'You are quite pale today, papa.' But papa kept silent and [now comes the parody of a Bible parable!] he told none of what had befallen him, nor where he had been, nor whither he had wished to go. The whole occurrence made a very strong impression on him [here begins the down-hill slide, that spectacular bathos which Gogol uses for his particular needs]. Much more seldom *even* did he address to his subordinates the words 'How dare you?— Do you know to whom you are speaking?'—or at least if he did talk that way it was not till he had first listened to what they had to tell. But still more remarkable was the fact that from that time on the ghostly clerk quite ceased to appear: evidently the Important Person's overcoat fitted him well; at least no more did one hear of overcoats being snatched from people's shoulders. However, many active and vigilant persons refused to be appeased and kept asserting that in remote parts of the city the ghostly clerk still showed himself. And indeed a suburban policeman saw with his own eyes [the downward slide from the moralistic note to the grotesque is now a tumble] a ghost appear from behind a house. But being by nature somewhat of a weakling (so that once, an ordinary full-grown young pig which had rushed out of some private house knocked him off his feet to the great merriment of a group of cab drivers from whom he demanded, and obtained, as a penalty for this derision, ten coppers from each to buy himself snuff), he did not venture to stop the ghost but just kept on walking behind it in the darkness, until the ghost suddenly turned, stopped and inquired: 'What d'you want, you?'—and showed a fist of a size rarely met with *even* among the living. 'Nothing,' answered the sentinel and proceeded to go back at once. That ghost, however, was a much taller one and had a huge moustache. It was heading apparently towards Obukhov Bridge and presently disappeared completely in the darkness of the night."

The torrent of "irrelevant" details (such as the bland assumption that "full-grown young pigs" commonly occur in private houses) produces such a hypnotic effect that one almost fails to realize one simple thing (and that is the beauty of the final stroke). A piece of most important information, the main structural idea of the story is here deliberately masked by Gogol (because all reality is a mask). The man taken for Akaky Akakyevich's cloakless ghost is actually the man who stole his cloak. But Akaky Akakyevich's ghost existed solely on the strength of his lacking a cloak, whereas now the policeman, lapsing into the queerest paradox of the story, mistakes for this ghost just the very person who was its antithesis, the man who had stolen the cloak. Thus the story describes a full circle: a vicious circle as all circles are, despite their posing as apples, or planets, or human faces.

So to sum up: the story goes this way: mumble, mumble, lyrical wave, mumble, lyrical wave, mumble, lyrical wave, mumble, fantastic climax, mumble, mumble, and back into the chaos from which they all had derived. At this superhigh level of art, literature is of course not concerned with pitying the underdog or cursing the upperdog. It appeals to that secret depth of the human soul where the shadows of other worlds pass like the shadows of nameless and soundless ships.

6

As one or two patient readers may have gathered by now, this is really the only appeal that interests me. My purpose in jotting these notes on Gogol has, I hope, become perfectly clear. Bluntly speaking it amounts to the following: if you expect to find out something about Russia, if you are eager to know why the blistered Germans bungled their blitz, if you are interested in "ideas" and "facts" and "messages," keep away from Gogol. The awful trouble of learning Russian in order to read him will not be repaid in your kind of hard cash. Keep away, keep away. He has nothing to tell you. Keep off the tracks. High tension. Closed for the duration. Avoid, refrain, don't. I would like to have here a full list of all possible interdictions, vetoes and threats. Hardly necessary of course—as the wrong sort of reader will certainly never get as far as this. But I do welcome the right sort—my brothers, my doubles. My brother is playing the organ. My sister is reading. She is my aunt. You will first learn the alphabet, the labials, the linguals, the dentals, the letters that buzz, the drone and the bumblebee, and the Tse-tse Fly. One of the vowels will make you say "Ugh!" You will feel mentally stiff and bruised after your first declension of personal pronouns. I see however no other way of getting to Gogol (or to any other Russian writer for that matter). His work, as all great literary achievements, is a phenomenon of language and not one of ideas. "Gaw-gol," not "Go-gall." The final "l" is a soft dissolving "l" which does not exist in English. One cannot hope to understand an author if one cannot even pronounce his name. My translations of various passages are the best my poor vocabulary could afford, but even had they been as perfect as those which I hear with my innermost ear, without being able to render their intonation, they still would not replace Gogol. While trying to convey my attitude towards his art I have not produced any tangible proofs of its peculiar existence. I can only place my hand on my heart and affirm that I have not imagined Gogol. He really wrote, he really lived.

Gogol was born on the 1st of April, 1809. According to his mother (who, of course, made up the following dismal anecdote) a poem he had written at the age of five was seen by Kapnist, a well-known writer of sorts. Kapnist embraced the solemn urchin and said to the glad parents: "He will become a writer of genius if only destiny gives him a good Christian for teacher and guide." But the other thing—his having been born on the 1st of April— is true.

6. COMMENTARIES

—"WELL,"—SAID MY PUBLISHER. . . .
A delicate sunset was framed in a golden gap between gaunt mountains. The remote rims of the gap were eyelashed with firs and still further, deep in the gap itself, one could distinguish the silhouettes of other, lesser and quite ethereal, mountains. We were in Utah, sitting in the lounge of an Alpine hotel. The slender aspens on the near slopes and the pale pyramids of ancient mine dumps took advantage of the plateglass window to participate silently in our talk—somewhat in the same way as the Byronic pictures did in regard to the dialogue in Sobakevich's house.

—"Well,"—said my publisher,—"I like it—but I do think the student ought to be told what it is all about."

I said . . .

—"No,"—he said,—"I don't mean that. I mean the student ought to be told more about Gogol's books. I mean the *plots*. He would want to know what those books are *about*."

I said . . .

—"No, you have not,"—he said.—"I have gone through it carefully and so has my wife, and we have not found the plots. There should also be some kind of bibliography or chronology at the end. The student ought to be able to find his way, otherwise he would be puzzled and would not bother to read any further."

I said that an intelligent person could always look up dates and things in a good encyclopedia or in any manual of Russian literature. He said that a student would not be necessarily an intelligent person and anyway would resent the trouble of having to look up things. I said there were students and students. He said that from a publisher's point of view there was only one sort.

—"I have tried to explain,"—I said,—"that in Gogol's books the real plots are behind the obvious ones. Those real plots I do give. His stories only mimic stories with plots. It is like a rare moth that departs from a moth-like appearance to mimic the superficial pattern of a structurally quite different thing—some popular butterfly, say."

—"That's all right,"—he said.

—"Or rather unpopular, unpopular with lizards and birds."

—"Yes, I understand,"—he said.—"I understand perfectly well. But after all a plot is a plot, and the student must be told what *happens*. For instance, until I read *The Government Inspector* myself I had not the slightest idea what it was all about although I had studied your manuscript."

—"Tell me,"—I asked,—"what happens in *The Inspector General?*"

—"Well,"—he said, throwing himself back in his chair, —"what happens is that a young man gets stranded in a town because he had lost all his money at cards, and the town is full of politicians, and he uses the politicians to raise some money by making them believe that he is a Government official sent from headquarters to inspect them. And when he has used them, and made love to the Mayor's daughter, and drunk the Mayor's wine, and accepted bribes from judges and doctors and landowners and merchants and all kinds of administrators, he leaves the town, just before the real inspector arrives."

I said—

—"Yes, of course you may use it,"—said my publisher cooperatively.—"Then there is also *Dead Souls*. I could not tell what it is all about after reading your chapter. And then, as I say, there ought to be a bibliography."

—"If you mean a list of translations and books on Gogol . . ."

—"Well,"—said my publisher.

—"If you want that, the matter is simple, for except Guerney's excellently rendered *Dead Souls, The Inspector General* and *The Overcoat*, which appeared while I was myself wrestling with them, there exists nothing but ridiculously garbled versions."

At this point two cocker puppies, a draggle-eared black one with an appealing slant in the bluish whites of his eyes and a little white bitch with a pink-dappled face and belly, tumbled in through the door someone had opened, stumbled about on padded paws in between the furniture and were promptly caught and banished again to their place on the terrace.

153

—"Otherwise,"—I went on,—"I know of no English work on Gogol worth listing except Mirsky's excellent chapter in his *History of Russian Literature* (Knopf, New York). Of course, there are hundreds of *Russian* works. Of these a few are very good, but lots of others belong to the preposterous schools of "Gogol the Painter of Tsarist Russia" or "Gogol the Realist" or "Gogol the Great Opposer of Serfdom and Bureaucracy" or 'Gogol the Russian Dickens." The trouble is that if I start listing these works, I am sure to try to allay my boredom by inserting here and there fictitious titles and imaginary authors so that you will never quite know whether Dobrolubov or Ivanov-Razumnik or Ovsyano Kuli—"

—"No,"—said my publisher hastily.—"I don't think that a list of books on Gogol is necessary. What I meant, was a list of Gogol's own books with a sequence of dates and a chronology of his doings, and something about the plots and so on. You could easily do this. And we must have Gogol's picture."

—"I have been thinking of that myself,"—I said. "Yes— let us have a picture of Gogol's nose. Not his face and shoulders, etc. but only his nose. A big solitary sharp nose —neatly outlined in ink like the enlarged figure of some important part of a curious zoological specimen. I might ask Dobuzhinsky, that unique master of the line, or perhaps a Museum artist . . ."

—"And it would kill the book,"—said my publisher.

That is how the following pages got appended. This chronology is meant for the indolent reader who wants to take in Gogol's life and labors at a glance instead of wallowing through my book in search of this or that relevant passage. Such passages are referred to in the chronology. The picture is the one described in the text and is reproduced from Veressaiev's delightful biography of Gogol (1933, in Russian). Most of my facts are taken from the same convenient work—for instance Gogol's long letter to his mother and such things. The deductions are my own. Desperate Russian critics, trying hard to find an Influence and to pigeonhole my own novels, have once or twice linked me up with Gogol, but when they looked again I had untied the knots and the box was empty.

NIKOLAI VASSILIEVICH GOGOL CHRONOLOGY

April 1st *1809*	Born in the bright and muddy market town of Soro-chintzy (stress accent on "chintz"), Province of Poltava, Little Russia (*see page 7*).
1821	Matriculated (Nezhin High School) (*page 8*).
1825	His father, a small landowner and an amateur Ukrainian playwright, died.
1828	Graduated and went to St. Petersburg. The distance is from 50° to 60°, i.e. the same as from Vancouver to Caribou. That year Tolstoy was born in the Province of Tula.
1829	Desultory job-hunting and publication of two poems, the lyric *Italy* and what he dubbed "an idyll," the long and indifferent *Hanz Kuechelgarten* (*page 9*).
August 1st *1829*	Burnt all the copies of *Hanz* (*page 10*).
August–Sept. *1829*	Freak journey to Northern Germany (*page 23*). Flitted back and entered the Civil Service (*page 26*).
1830	Began contributing short stories of Ukrainian life to literary reviews (*page 26*).

CHRONOLOGY

1831	Flitted out of the cob-webbed gloom of Civil Service and began teaching history at a young ladies' institute. The girls found him dull.
End of May 1831	Met Pushkin. (Alexander Pushkin, 1799–1837, the greatest Russian poet) (*page 29*).
September 1831	Published first volume of *Evenings on a Farm near Dikanka*, a collection of short stories dealing with ghosts and Ukrainians, and still considered by some critics to be very racy and full of fun (*page 29*).
March 1832	Second volume of the above. There is a famous description of the Dniepr in the story *The Awful Vengeance* ("Fair is the Dniepr in windless weather, etc.") and a touch of the real Gogol to come, in *Ivan Shponka and his Aunt* (*page 32*).
1834	Was appointed through literary friends to the post of Assistant Professor of World History at the University of St. Petersburg. His first lecture, which he had carefully prepared, successfully concealed his meager erudition under the rotund waves of his poetical eloquence. Subsequently he used to appear with his cheek bandaged up so as to imply a swollen jaw hampering speech and dejectedly dealt out and distributed among his students little pictures of Roman ruins.
1835	Published two volumes of stories entitled *Mirgorod*, containing: *Viy*, a gooseflesh story, not particularly effective; *The Old-World Landowners*, where "the vegetable humors of the old pair, their sloth, their gluttony, their selfishness, are idealized and sentimentalized" (Mirsky: *History of Russian Literature*, page 194); the *Story of the Quarrel between Ivan Ivanovich and Ivan Nikiforovich* which he had read to Pushkin on December 2nd 1833 ("very original and very funny"—Pushkin's comment) and which is the best of his purely humorous tales; and *Taras Bulba*, a melodramatic account of the adventures of quite fictitious cossacks—something like the *Cid*

of Corneille and his Spaniards (or Hemingway's Spaniards, for that matter) in a Ukrainian disguise. The same year he published a volume of essays and stories, *Arabesques*, among which are the *Nevsky Avenue* (*page 12*), the *Memoirs of a Madman* (see concluding passage: *page vi*) and *The Portrait*—a portrait coming to life—that kind of thing. About the same time he wrote his remarkable nightmare *The Nose*, the story of an unfortunate person, whose nose went off on its own in the aspect of a man about town (as in dreams when you know that somebody is so-and-so, but are not disturbed by his looking like somebody else or like nothing at all) (*page 4*) and two plays: *Revizor* (*The Government Inspector*) (*page 35*), and *Getting Married* —a rather slipshod comedy about the hesitations of a man who has made up his mind to marry, has a swallowtail coat made, is provided with a fiancée— but at the last moment makes a fenestral exit. None of Gogol's heroes could get very far with women.

December 18th *1835*	"We spat at each other and parted, I and the University. I am again a carefree cossack." (from a letter to Pogodin).
January 30th *1836*	Read his new play *The Government Inspector* at one of Zhoukovsky's soirées. (Zhoukovsky, 1783–1878, leader of the "romantic movement," the great translator of German and English poetry).
May 1st *1836*	First performance of *The Government Inspector* (*page 37*).
June *1836*	Left in a huff for foreign lands (*page 57*). "Henceforward for twelve years (1836–48) he lived abroad, coming to Russia for short periods only." (Mirsky: page 186).
October *1836*	Vevey, Switzerland. Here he really began writing the First Part of *Dead Souls*, which had been planned out some time in May in St. Petersburg.

CHRONOLOGY

Winter *1836–1837*	Paris. Lived on the corner of the Place de la Bourse and rue Vivienne. Wrote there a large portion of the First Part of *Dead Souls*. Browning's door is preserved in the library of Wellesley College. On warmish days he took Chichikov for strolls in the Tuileries. Sparrows, grey statues.
Beginning of *1837*	Rome. "My life, my supreme delectation has died with him." (letter to Pogodin after Pushkin's duel and death in St. Petersburg).
Spring *1838*	Rome. Two Polish Catholics thought—judging by their reports to headquarters—that they were very successfully converting Gogol. The critic Veressaiev (*Gogol v. Zhisni*, Moscow-Leningrad, 1933. Academia: page 190) suggests however that Gogol was rather nastily deceiving the good men whom he dropped as soon as his rich and useful friend Princess Zinaida Volkonsky (an ardent Catholic) had left Rome.
May *1839*	A brief romantic friendship with young Prince Vielgorsky who was dying of tuberculosis in Rome. The hours spent at the young man's bedside have their vibrant echo in the pathos of Gogol's short piece *Nights in a Villa*.
Winter *1839–1840*	Return to Russia. Read the first chapters of *Dead Souls* to his literary friends.
April *1840*	"A person not having his own carriage would like to find a traveling companion having one for a journey to Vienna. Expenses shared." (Advertisement in *Moscow Gazette*).
June 1840– *October 1841*	Back in Italy. Was much together with Russian painters who worked in Rome. Completed *The Overcoat* (*page 139*).
Winter *1841–1842*	Back in Russia.
1842	Published First Part of *Dead Souls* (*page 61*). In Gogol's day you could, if you were a Russian land-

owner, sell peasants, buy peasants and mortgage peasants. Peasants were termed "souls" as cattle is reckoned by "heads." If you then happened to mention that you had a hundred souls, you would mean not that you were a minor poet, but that you were a small squire. The Government checked the number of your peasants, as you had to pay a poll tax for them. If any of your peasants died you would still have to go on paying until the next census. The dead "soul" was still on the list. You could no longer use the mobile physical appendages it had had once, such as arms or legs, but the soul you had lost was still alive in the Elysium of official paperdom and only another census could obliterate it. The immortality of the soul lasted for a few seasons, but you had to pay for it all the time. Chichikov's plan in *Dead Souls* was to acquire those unavoidably accumulating dead souls from you, so that he, not you, would be paying the tax. He thought you would be glad to get rid of them and overjoyed if you got a small bonus from him for the transaction. After he had collected a sufficient number of these ridiculously cheap souls, he intended to mortgage them, as good live souls, which they nominally were according to official documents. As I suggest (*page 72*) a Government which allowed the traffic of live souls, that is live human beings, could be hardly expected to act as an ethical expert in a business involving merely the traffic of dead souls—abstract nicknames on a scrap of paper. This point Gogol completely missed when in the second part of *Dead Souls* he attempted to treat Chichikov as a human sinner and the Government as a superhuman judge. All the characters in the first part being equally subhuman, and all living in the bosom of Gogol's demonocracy, it does not matter a damn who judges whom.

CHRONOLOGY

Chichikov is shown coming to the town of N. and making friends with its worthies. He then visits the neighboring squires and more or less cheaply gets his dead souls from them. The sequence of his deals takes him to solemn, thick-backed Sobakevich; to mild lackadaisical Manilov; to covetous, moth-eaten Plushkin, pronounced "plew-shkin," as if the moth had made a hole in the plush; to Dame Korobochka, who is a perfect mixture of the superstitious and the matter-of-fact; and to the bully Nozdryov, who is a nasty noisy nosey swindler and not a pleasant one as Paul Chichikov is. The former's chatter and Korobochka's wariness turn the town against our plump adventurer, our necrophilous Casanova, our rolling stone, our Mr. Chichikov. He leaves the town on the wings of one of those wonderful lyrical interpolations, which the author inserts (landscape, expanded metaphor, conjuror's patter) every time his hero is on his way between two business interviews. For discussion of the texture of *Dead Souls* see pages 61–113.

Of the Second Part of the novel we have only the first chapters. A few more squires are interviewed and finally Chichikov gets into some real trouble with the police. Good as some passages are, the author's spiritual message is felt to be gradually killing the book (*page 132*).

1842–1848	Travels from place to place seeking health, inspiration, finding neither.
1847	Published *Selected Passages from Correspondence with Friends* (*page 126*).
Spring 1848	Dim pilgrimage to Palestine (*page 130*).
1848–1852	Moscow, Odessa, Vassilievka (his mother's home), monasteries, Moscow again.
February 1852	"Renounce Pushkin! He was a sinner and a pagan." said fierce, healthy Father Matthew to limp, sick Gogol during their last meeting.

161

February 11th
1852

"That night Gogol prayed for a long time alone in his room. At 3 a.m. he called his servant boy and wanted to know whether the rooms on the other side of the house were warm [he was staying in the Moscow house of Count A. P. Tolstoy, a fanatic follower of Father M.] The boy answered they were not. 'Give me a cloak,' said Gogol, 'and come on, I have some business there.' He went, carrying a candle, and making the sign of a cross in every room he passed through. In one of them he ordered the boy to open the flue as softly as possible so as not to awaken anybody and then asked for a certain portfolio that lay in a chest-of-drawers. When the portfolio was brought he took out a batch of copybooks tied together with a ribbon, put them into the stove and set fire to the papers by means of his candle. The boy [so Pogodin tells us in his account of the burning of the Second and Third Parts of *Dead Souls*] understanding what was happening, fell on his knees and implored him to desist. 'None of your business,' said Gogol, 'better pray.' The boy began to sob and continued to plead with him. Gogol noticed that the fire was going out—that only the corners of the copybooks had been charred. So he took out the bundle, undid the ribbon, placed the papers in such a way as to facilitate combustion, tipped his candle again and then sat down on a chair beside the fire, waiting for the papers to be consumed. When it was all over, he crossed himself, went back to his room, kissed the boy, lay down on a couch and broke into tears." A feeling of relief may have been mingled with the sense of disaster (*page 131*).

March 4th
1852

Died (*page 1*).

INDEX

INDEX

INDEX

INDEX

169

INDEX

VLADIMIR NABOKOV

"I WAS BORN ON THE 23RD OF APRIL 1899 IN ST. PETERSBURG, Russia. My grandfather was Minister of Justice to Alexander II. My father was a well-known statesman of the Liberal group, a professor of Criminal Law, and a Member of the First Russian Parliament.

"I attended the Tenishev School in St. Petersburg. After leaving Russia in 1919, I went to Cambridge University, Trinity College, where (in 1922) I obtained a "first class" degree in Foreign Languages (French, Medieval and Modern, and Russian).

"From 1922 to 1937 I lived in Berlin, Germany, where my main occupation was writing. I also taught languages and had numerous private pupils.

"In 1937, I saw myself obliged to leave Germany and went to France. In May 1940, I emigrated to the United States, where I first taught Russian Literature at Wellesley College and then, from 1948 to 1959, Russian and European Literature at Cornell University.

"I am married since 1925 and have a son.

"My life-long hobby is lepidopterology. I am also a chess problem composer. I am good at games, especially at tennis."

After resigning from Cornell University in 1959, Nabokov has travelled abroad and worked in California on the screenplay of his novel *Lolita*. In addition to such celebrated novels as *Laughter in the Dark, The Real Life of Sebastian Knight, Lolita* and *Invitation to a Beheading*, he has published volumes of short stories, poetry and translations. His five-volume edition of Pushkin's *Eugen Onegin* was published by the Bollingen Foundation.

ALSO BY VLADIMIR NABOKOV

Laughter in the Dark

"Once upon a time there lived in Berlin, Germany, a man called Albinus. He was rich, respectable, happy; one day he abandoned his wife for the sake of a youthful mistress; he loved; was not loved; and his life ended in disaster." This, Nabokov tells us, at the beginning of the book, is the whole story; nothing more—except that he starts from here, with dazzling skill and irony, *and* sixteen-year-old Margot (precursor of Lolita?) to construct a chilling, original tale of folly and destruction. Originally published 1938.

"... a remarkable achievement, if not a masterpiece."
—*New York Times*

"A first-rate thriller with clever psychological trimmings and an atmosphere combining Chekhovian lassitude with surrealist degeneracy."—Clifton Fadiman, *The New Yorker*.

The Real Life of Sebastian Knight

A novel about an imaginary writer, a brilliant piece of literary detection and at the same time a profound discussion of the role of the artist in modern society and the problem of human identity.

"A brilliantly written investigation ... The humor is both sardonic and delicate. Its comments on the art of writing would alone recommend the book."—Wallace Fowlie

"... one of his best performances."—F. W. Dupee

"*The Real Life of Sebastian Knight,* like everything Nabokov writes, has great beauty and power."—Flannery O'Connor

Published by New Directions

New Directions Paperbooks — a partial listing

Martín Adán, The Cardboard House
César Aira
  An Episode in the Life of a Landscape Painter
  Ghosts
  The Literary Conference
Will Alexander, The Sri Lankan Loxodrome
Paul Auster, The Red Notebook
Gennady Aygi, Child-and-Rose
Honoré de Balzac, Colonel Chabert
Djuna Barnes, Nightwood
Charles Baudelaire, The Flowers of Evil*
Bei Dao, The Rose of Time: New & Selected Poems*
Nina Berberova, The Ladies From St. Petersburg
Rafael Bernal, The Mongolian Conspiracy
Roberto Bolaño, By Night in Chile
  Distant Star
  Last Evenings on Earth
  Nazi Literature in the Americas
Jorge Luis Borges, Labyrinths
  Seven Nights
Coral Bracho, Firefly Under the Tongue*
Kamau Brathwaite, Ancestors
Sir Thomas Browne, Urn Burial
Basil Bunting, Complete Poems
Anne Carson, Glass, Irony & God
Horacio Castellanos Moya, Senselessness
Louis-Ferdinand Céline
  Death on the Installment Plan
  Journey to the End of the Night
René Char, Selected Poems
Inger Christensen, alphabet
Jean Cocteau, The Holy Terrors
Peter Cole, Things on Which I've Stumbled
Julio Cortázar, Cronopios & Famas
Albert Cossery, The Colors of Infamy
Robert Creeley, If I Were Writing This
Guy Davenport, 7 Greeks
Osamu Dazai, The Setting Sun
H.D., Tribute to Freud
  Trilogy
Helen DeWitt, Lightning Rods
Robert Duncan, Groundwork
  Selected Poems
Eça de Queirós, The Maias
William Empson, 7 Types of Ambiguity
Shusaku Endo, Deep River
  The Samurai
Jenny Erpenbeck, Visitation

Lawrence Ferlinghetti
  A Coney Island of the Mind
Thalia Field, Bird Lovers, Backyard
F. Scott Fitzgerald, The Crack-Up
  On Booze
Forrest Gander, As a Friend
  Core Samples From the World
Romain Gary, The Life Before Us (Mme. Rosa)
Henry Green, Pack My Bag
Allen Grossman, Descartes' Loneliness
John Hawkes, The Lime Twig
Felisberto Hernández, Lands of Memory
Hermann Hesse, Siddhartha
Takashi Hiraide
  For the Fighting Spirit of the Walnut*
Yoel Hoffman, The Christ of Fish
Susan Howe, My Emily Dickinson
  That This
Bohumil Hrabal, I Served the King of England
Sonallah Ibrahim, That Smell
Christopher Isherwood, The Berlin Stories
Fleur Jaeggy, Sweet Days of Discipline
Gustav Janouch, Conversations With Kafka
Alfred Jarry, Ubu Roi
B.S. Johnson, House Mother Normal
Franz Kafka, Amerika: The Man Who Disappeared
Alexander Kluge, Cinema Stories
Laszlo Krasznahorkai, Satantango
  The Melancholy of Resistance
Mme. de Lafayette, The Princess of Clèves
Lautréamont, Maldoror
Denise Levertov, Selected Poems
  Tesserae
Li Po, Selected Poems
Clarice Lispector, The Hour of the Star
  Near to the Wild Heart
  The Passion According to G. H.
Luljeta Lleshanaku, Child of Nature
Federico García Lorca, Selected Poems*
  Three Tragedies
Nathaniel Mackey, Splay Anthem
Stéphane Mallarmé, Selected Poetry and Prose*
Javier Marías, Your Face Tomorrow (3 volumes)
  While the Women Are Sleeping
Thomas Merton, New Seeds of Contemplation
  The Way of Chuang Tzu
Henri Michaux, Selected Writings
Dunya Mikhail, Diary of a Wave Outside the Sea

Henry Miller, The Air-Conditioned Nightmare
  Big Sur & The Oranges of Hieronymus Bosch
  The Colossus of Maroussi
Yukio Mishima, Confessions of a Mask
  Death in Midsummer
Eugenio Montale, Selected Poems*
Vladimir Nabokov, Laughter in the Dark
  Nikolai Gogol
  The Real Life of Sebastian Knight
Pablo Neruda, The Captain's Verses*
  Love Poems*
  Residence on Earth*
Charles Olson, Selected Writings
George Oppen, New Collected Poems (with CD)
Wilfred Owen, Collected Poems
Michael Palmer, Thread
Nicanor Parra, Antipoems*
Boris Pasternak, Safe Conduct
Kenneth Patchen
  Memoirs of a Shy Pornographer
Octavio Paz, Selected Poems
  A Tale of Two Gardens
Victor Pelevin
  The Hall of the Singing Caryatids
  Omon Ra
Saint-John Perse, Selected Poems
Ezra Pound, The Cantos
  New Selected Poems and Translations
  Personae
Raymond Queneau, Exercises in Style
Qian Zhongshu, Fortress Besieged
Raja Rao, Kanthapura
Herbert Read, The Green Child
Kenneth Rexroth, Songs of Love, Moon & Wind
  Written on the Sky: Poems from the Japanese
Keith Ridgway, Hawthorn & Child
Rainer Maria Rilke
  Poems from the Book of Hours
Arthur Rimbaud, Illuminations*
  A Season in Hell and The Drunken Boat*
Guillermo Rosales, The Halfway House
Evelio Rosero, The Armies
  Good Offices
Joseph Roth, The Emperor's Tomb
Jerome Rothenberg, Triptych
Ihara Saikaku, The Life of an Amorous Woman
William Saroyan
  The Daring Young Man on the Flying Trapeze
Albertine Sarrazin, Astragal

Jean-Paul Sartre, Nausea
  The Wall
Delmore Schwartz
  In Dreams Begin Responsibilities
W. G. Sebald, The Emigrants
  The Rings of Saturn
  Vertigo
Aharon Shabtai, J'accuse
Hasan Shah, The Dancing Girl
C. H. Sisson, Selected Poems
Gary Snyder, Turtle Island
Muriel Spark, The Ballad of Peckham Rye
  A Far Cry From Kensington
  Memento Mori
George Steiner, My Unwritten Books
Antonio Tabucchi, Indian Nocturne
  Pereira Declares
Yoko Tawada, The Bridegroom Was a Dog
  The Naked Eye
Dylan Thomas, A Child's Christmas in Wales
  Collected Poems
  Under Milk Wood
Uwe Timm, The Invention of Curried Sausage
Charles Tomlinson, Selected Poems
Tomas Tranströmer
  The Great Enigma: New Collected Poems
Leonid Tsypkin, The Bridge over the Neroch
  Summer in Baden-Baden
Tu Fu, Selected Poems
Frederic Tuten, The Adventures of Mao
Paul Valéry, Selected Writings
Enrique Vila-Matas, Bartleby & Co.
  Dublinesque
Elio Vittorini, Conversations in Sicily
Rosmarie Waldrop, Driven to Abstraction
Robert Walser, The Assistant
  Microscripts
  The Tanners
Eliot Weinberger, An Elemental Thing
  Oranges and Peanuts for Sale
Nathanael West
  Miss Lonelyhearts & The Day of the Locust
Tennessee Williams, Cat on a Hot Tin Roof
  The Glass Menagerie
  A Streetcar Named Desire
William Carlos Williams, In the American Grain
  Selected Poems
  Spring and All
Louis Zukofsky, "A"
  Anew

*BILINGUAL EDITION

For a complete listing, request a free catalog from New Directions, 80 8th Avenue, NY NY 10011
or visit us online at ndbooks.com